GETTING
MESSY

GETTING MESSY

A GUIDE TO TAKING RISKS AND
OPENING THE IMAGINATION
FOR TEACHERS, TRAINERS, COACHES AND MENTORS

KIM HERMANSON, PH.D.

GETTING MESSY: A GUIDE TO TAKING RISKS AND OPENING THE IMAGINATION
FOR TEACHERS, TRAINERS, COACHES AND MENTORS

KIM HERMANSON, PH.D.

LIBRARY OF CONGRESS CONTROL NUMBER: 2009900910

ISBN-13: 978-0-578-01190-5

COVER AND INTERIOR DESIGN: THE BOOK DESIGNERS
INITIAL CONCEPT DESIGN: LESLIE LAUF
AUTHOR PHOTOGRAPH: SUSAN ADLER
PRODUCTION: THE BOOK DESIGNERS
PUBLISHER: RAWBERRY BOOKS
157 PARK STREET
SAN RAFAEL, CA 94901

TO CONTACT KIM HERMANSON:
KIM.HERMANSON@GMAIL.COM

Dedicated to the kindred souls
who love to learn and explore the unknown.

CONTENTS

PREFACE

GETTING MESSY was written for teachers, trainers, mentors, coaches, workshop leaders, and group facilitators. Parents, consultants, counselors, and others who work with people in meaningful ways will also find it helpful. I define the word "teaching" broadly to refer to any situation in which we are contributing to another person's experience. Certainly, if you are in a role that holds some sort of authority, you are teaching.

This book proposes a contrary view of teaching or leadership roles, and argues that when we consciously enter these situations as "learners" (whether it's a group of newly-trained therapists or a corporate seminar for high-level executives), we create space for a greater wisdom to speak. The philosopher Hannah Arendt called this space "an in-between," theologians define it as a "Divine Third," and Martin Buber named it "Thou." When we form a relationship with something (person, group, organization) we care about, that thing is no longer an "It." There is a depth that is present in the relationship—a sense of mystery. We are in relation to something that is "other" and it's clear that we don't have all the answers, we can't figure this out ahead of time. All we can do is put whatever we have to say out there, see what comes back, and use feedback to alter course. Working with other people in this way is a deeply creative process.

Acknowledging the "in between" space is essential, because we need to have space for the expansion of our knowing to happen. There is a greater intelligence that wishes to operate through us when we coach a client, lead a group, or hold a meeting. I have experienced the potential of this larger intelligence countless times. When I fully take on the stance of a learner to the process (no matter how much of an expert I am in a particular subject), I am open to a greater wisdom that always wants to come through.

In an earlier draft, I ended the Preface by saying that *Getting Messy* was a "work in progress." To me, the book asks more questions than it answers; it opens more doors than it closes. Working in the realm of "imaginal space," it likely couldn't be any other way. The content of this book points to avenues beyond what is currently known. A friend read my words and said they sounded liked an apology. She kindly reframed it: "Kim, this is *your life's work...in process.*" The inquiry continues.

CHAPTER ONE
Teaching is a Way of Growing

Here is Edward Bear, coming downstairs now, hump, bump, bump, on the back of his head behind Christopher Robin. It is, as far as he knows, the only way of coming downstairs, but sometimes he feels that there really is another way, if only he could stop bumping for a moment and think of it.

— A.A. MILNE, WINNIE THE POOH

1

EVERYTHING RESTS ON WHO YOU ARE

M Y WORKING LIFE has always been diverse. Over the past thirty years I've developed and taught seminars, worked as a coach and consultant, and facilitated many groups on an assortment of topics. My clientele have ranged from Senior citizens to troubled teenagers to creatively blocked adults and everything in between. I've developed and taught computer training courses for Fortune 500 corporations, led tours for wine connoisseurs at a local farmers market, facilitated creative writing workshops at a yoga center, organized focus groups for educational institutions, taught swimming lessons for children and grown adults, hosted community poetry readings at the public library, presented technical expertise at corporate meetings, and mentored troubled teens at a high-priced boarding school. I've also taught a range of university courses for undergraduate and graduate students. In all cases, diverse as they may be, the same principles of teaching and learning applied.

I didn't know this ten years ago when I was hired to teach an "Instructional Strategies" course in a teacher credentialing program. I presumed, of course, that teaching was about standing in front of a group of students as an expert, delivering content information. The problem I had, however, was that the roles were switched. My students, with a couple exceptions, were experienced teachers who simply needed to acquire a course credit and I—I had never taught a class in a formal classroom before. I wasn't even sure what instructional strategies were. I was frightened.

What did I do? I went on a search for tools and techniques. I wanted to know *how* to teach. I wanted someone to tell me everything I needed to know to be a good teacher. I would then memorize this information, practice it at home, and hope the students in my classes would never know that I was inexperienced. One of my first stops was a workshop on how to facilitate groups. However, on the third day of this five-day workshop, we still had not gotten to techniques. I still did not have anything to arm myself with when I walked into the classroom to teach for the first time. I was frustrated and when the workshop resumed after lunch I spoke up. "This isn't what I came here for. I need to know how to teach." The instructor looked at me for a moment and then turned around and drew this diagram on the flip chart:

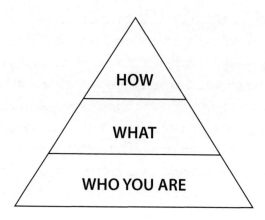

"Everything rests on who you are," he told me, "Once you have that, the 'how' is easy."

So I started teaching a classroom of experienced teachers with no techniques under my belt. The only real method I had was to be a learner, to try things out and learn along with the students whether they worked or not. After all, the title of the course was Instructional Strategies—what better way to learn than to use the course itself as our laboratory?

My class was a required course in a teacher-credentialing program at a large university, a program that provided teaching certificates to vocational and adult educators. Students came from dramatically diverse backgrounds and teaching situations, and most of them had been teaching for years. There were high school and junior high teachers, but also medical educators, corporate trainers, social workers, teachers who worked with disabled populations, in senior centers, prisons, nursing homes, and so on. It was clear that there was no way I could provide these people with a pre-packaged set of information. My task was to pursue a deeper inquiry into teaching along with my students. It would be an adventure.

I was not an expert on the subject of classroom teaching and I certainly couldn't offer these students specialized expertise regarding their own particular teaching situations. But I soon discovered that I had a skill that was much more important: *I was an expert learner.* I didn't need to present myself to the class as someone who had all the answers. My real job was to be a guide, to initiate with my students a conversation about the subject of teaching. I would enter into this inquiry along with the students and I would be fluid with whatever arose from that conversation. I would draw the wisdom out of the room and I would learn along the way. I have since come to discover that no matter what situation is in front of me, whether it be a group of rambunctious teens or weary adults, being a learner is the only thing that really works. Being a learner is what allows creative insight to happen.

The first time you give a presentation at a sales conference to a bunch of jaded sales reps can feel similarly. And the answer is the same. It doesn't work to try to "sell" them; what works is to be authentic. What works is to share with them what you feel genuinely enthusiastic about. They'll respond to your integrity. As Gertrude Stein once said, "No one real is boring."

Yet how often do we give ourselves the freedom to be real when we're working with other people in some professional capacity, especially when it involves the role or title of "expert"? Being real would mean that we sometimes make mistakes. Being real would mean that we are willing to take risks and experiment. Being real would mean that we're learners too.

TEACHING, LEARNING, AND IMAGINATION

IN THIS BOOK, I use the words *teacher* and *learner* broadly, to describe the capacities that we are engaging in when we work with other people in meaningful ways. We are involved in a teacher role when we are informally facilitating a group, coaching a youngster, or presenting information to colleagues. We take on the learner role when we work with a business coach to grow our business, attend a weight loss meeting, listen to an ad campaign, or speak with our partners. During the day we shift back and forth—sometimes teaching, sometimes learning. Healthy adults make this shift effortlessly.

No matter whether you facilitate groups, coach, mentor youngsters, or teach in a formal classroom, there are deeper principles of teaching and learning that apply across professional milieu, age groups, situations, and subject matters. These deeper principles of teaching and learning create the foundation for a transformative experience, moving the group beyond what you might have though possible. And the principles are universal, because what we are doing in all these situations is *connecting*—with some sort of subject, with ourselves, and with one another. Often, information needs to be conveyed. And even though the *content* of that information may vary, the principles that cause a Senior who is 20 years older than me to listen to what I have to say, are the same learning principles that keep teen-agers engaged. After all, we're all human.

Unfortunately, for most of us the words *teaching* and *learning* bring up memories of painful boredom. Like many of you, I've spent too much time in "learning" situations, trying to find ways to keep myself interested. If I can't find a way to stay engaged, I start drawing and doodling in my notebook; I make to-do lists, plan my weekend, daydream. Our standard model for teaching and learning is dry, boring, and mechanical. It's time we take teaching and learning out of the box and give them a little air. What I would like to know is this: *Why are most learning situations uninspired and unimaginative? Why are most so dull we count the minutes until we can get out of that room?* It doesn't have to be that way. Teaching and learning are two of the most important things we do in life. They make our lives exciting, interesting, and enjoyable. Teaching and learning are what make life worth living.

Most of us prepare to teach or lead groups by seeking out strategies and activities. We focus on perfecting our procedures and designing flawless presentations. We're concerned about the timing of activities and we nearly always define our responsibilities in terms of the required content to be taught. In the process, we reduce our work to the superficial level of technique. Our main concerns have become: *How do I silence the person who always asks odd questions?* Or, *Do I have time to review all this material at our next meeting?* For many of us, teaching, coaching, or leading a group has become a matter of problem solving, programming the event to work as efficiently as possible.

But let's look back on your experiences in school. What do you actually *remember?* I often pose this question to students. If they remember anything at all, what they remember are moments of *connection* with a teacher, a favorite subject or assignment, or fellow students. They remember teachers who were real people, who shared themselves, their lives, and their loves with them. They remember teachers who moved them, somehow managing to penetrate through their aloof and skeptical exteriors. Real teaching is somewhat mysterious. There's a depth to it that can't be explained. Clearly, it's not about techniques.

The tools-and-techniques approach suggests that our work with people is end-oriented, performance-oriented, that once we have the proper tools in our arsenal, we're done. However, activities and exercises by themselves have nothing to do with good teaching. The most highly skilled presenters are often the most boring and lifeless. Why? Because they hide behind their methods. The tools—the carefully timed break-out sessions, the detailed agendas, glossy handouts, slick PowerPoint presentations—have become central, replacing real connection.

People are human beings and human beings don't operate in predictable, machine-like ways. When our carefully-crafted exercises fail to work, we wonder why. We wonder why clients fail to understand us, why they're ornery, difficult, and belligerent. Most of all, we wonder why we've lost passion for our work. I'll tell you my reason: The core of teaching isn't about presenting information and learning has little to do with swallowing it.

Both Carl Jung and Albert Einstein said in different ways that no fundamental problem can ever be solved at the level at which it was created. To come up with new solutions, we need a larger context, a larger set of possibilities, and expanded ways of thinking. In other words, we need imagination. This is true for learning, as well. We can't learn anything unless we first imagine it possible. When we learn, we step out beyond what we know, into the arena of what we don't know. We are necessarily involved in a relationship with something that is larger than ourselves.

THE SOUL OF TEACHING

WHO YOU ARE is on display when you teach. Every issue you have—self-consciousness, fear, grief, boredom, hostility toward some unknown aggressor, embarrassment, likes, and dislikes—is on display for your clientele to notice. Consciously or unconsciously, they can *see* who you are, so you might as well use this as an opportunity to grow. The way many of us react to this unwanted vulnerability is to put up a wall between us and our clients. It's true that a certain level of professional distance is appropriate, but when the wall becomes too rigid and heavy, it blocks the authentic connection that can inspire learning for both teacher and learner. When we choose the path of growth, we view our work as sacred territory, being open to what occurs and working through what comes up for us—issue by issue.

When we work with others in a leadership or teaching capacity, it's interesting how frequently we remove *ourselves* from the learning process. But how can we expect to change others and remain unchanged ourselves? How can we expect to create a dynamic atmosphere of inquiry for our participants, yet be an observer to it? The more we separate ourselves from the messy business of learning, the more we lose heart for our work. We start to forget that we feel most alive when we're simply offering *ourselves*—our knowledge, passions, interests—to our students, clients, participants, colleagues. These very human qualities are what inspire others to learn from us. They're what cause people to keep coming back for more.

These are some of the things I learned when I stood, on shaky legs, and "taught" this group of experienced teachers. I assigned final papers to the students and below is one excerpt. The man who wrote it teaches auto mechanics in a vocational education program. He was a big, burly guy and was quiet in class. Of all my students, I thought he would be someone focused on the "mechanics" of teaching, rather than the "soul." I was wrong.

> I have gained much from reflection upon what I stand for and why I do what I do. I realize that I teach with the whole of my being, both lessons that are articulated and some that are not...I have always felt to a degree that students could sound the depths of my knowledge and commitment regardless of my physical actions. It is more than just body language, but communication on a much different level. *I know that they know.* How many times have you attended a seminar, only to leave unfulfilled, knowing that the facilitator was full of BS? Was it his mannerisms, his body language or the light of his aura? No matter how you knew, the fact is that *you knew.* Critical reflection has flowered my awareness. We teach who we are, with continuity, vision and purpose to what we are doing. If nothing else, I can shine my spirit, and teach with all the illumination and clarity that is within me. This is the most treasured lesson I will carry from this class.

No matter your particular subject, mode of delivery, or client population, who you are *matters.* The content of your agenda is the least significant thing that you are teaching. As Dale Carnegie once said, "What we are speaks more loudly than what we say. Sincerity, integrity, modesty and unselfishness affect an audience deeply." Whether you are presenting to a large audience or mentoring a youngster, what you are offering is deeper than your words or techniques. What you are offering is your Self.

Human learning does not happen at the level of technique or strategy. Learning doesn't require polished slides, a detailed agenda, or clear objectives. Learning involves being able to *connect*—with one another, with oneself, and with a subject. Human beings have a fundamental need to connect. How do we make and nurture these connections? How do we really learn from another person? How do we learn in a group? What are the things that inspire and provoke our learning? What are the things that motivate us to continue? And what stops us? Those are some of the questions we will be exploring in this book.

Diving below the level of technique, we investigate the elements that spark learning, including the rich arena of human interaction and communication. The metaphor that comes to mind is the image of a fertile field, full of expansive possibility. The fertile field supports *life*—plants can't grow or live without its rich soil. Human learning comes from fertile soil, as well. When we focus on our innovative techniques, we overlook this deeper dimension which is rich, messy, and hard to put into words. Something shifts inside us and all of a sudden we're moved, inspired, enthralled. The fertile field may look empty, but it's not.

Yes, of course we sign up for seminars and workshops to gain specialized information—to learn how to invest in the stock market, how to market our product on the Internet, or to receive a professional credential. Of course, there are numerous things we need to learn in order to be productive citizens and have successful lives. However, in the process of striving for these goals, we've forgotten how to be human with one another. We miss the expansive possibilities that happen when groups come together in meaningful ways. We focus on techniques and expertise, and miss the life. We focus on end results and miss the adventure.

No matter what sort of teaching you do, you have expertise. However, being an expert and being able to teach others are two different things. Your human qualities are what make you a teacher, because the base of teaching is who you are. In this book, we go back to that base. If you are an inexperienced teacher, you will begin to develop your teaching voice; if you are seasoned, you will discover a new connection to self that may have been submerged. As Ralph Waldo Emerson once said: That which you are, you will teach.

LEARNING IS MESSY

WHEN I WAS WORKING on this book, a friend of mine told me that he *hated* my title. He didn't want anything to do with *messy*. His life was spent keeping disorder at bay. But if recent books such as *A Perfect Mess: The Hidden Benefits of Disorder* are any indication, I believe that messiness is becoming more in vogue. People are starting to notice that perfectly ordered systems are both uncreative and inflexible.

Messiness presents us with the opportunity to create something new and experience something we wouldn't normally experience. When the blue pastel is left out on the table by mistake, for example, it invites us to create something with it. Or remember the days when journals weren't computerized? If we wanted to find a piece of information about something, we had to sort through stacks of books and magazines until we found what we were looking for. In the process, however, we encountered all sorts of odd, but surprisingly useful, information. Such synchronicities often produced amazing creative work, solved difficult problems, and generally provided delight.

For me, messy means exploring unknown territory and asking questions that take us outside of our current ways of knowing. It means that we don't have prepared answers; it may mean moments of awkward silence. When we appreciate and honor the deep mystery of the unknown, we develop patience, learning to wait until the right thing to do next emerges. All in all, human learning is messy...and that's the invitation. It's only when we step out of the mold and allow a little disarray, that learning and growth begin to happen.

It's true that there are models of learning that look quite neat and simple. Take memorizing, for example. Information is presented to us, we memorize it, and we spit it back out at the appropriate time. That is an orderly and perhaps favorable method of learning in our achievement-oriented society. Learning that is more transformational and lasting requires that we connect with deeper levels of wisdom and understanding—a process that could be called "discernment." Discernment requires a deeper connection to ourselves and it requires that we be able to *see* on a deeper level. We have to be able to look under the surface of things.

The groundbreaking research in "emotional intelligence" has clearly demonstrated the importance of wholeness in learning. We know now that learning is deeper than mere cognition. Learning involves accessing our own unique insights and our own emotions. Feelings are a fundamental aspect of learning; they are a signal that learning is happening. We are not learning anything of much significance if we don't feel *something*—excitement, wonder, anger, awe, fear—as part of the process.

I often use the word "sacred" in this book to describe the quality of the environment that best supports learning. Although one might sneer at the idea of sacredness in a professional setting, ignoring a sense of sacredness has been a gross disservice to teaching and learning. Parker Palmer, author of several books including *The Courage to Teach*, says that sacredness is that which is worthy of respect. Sacredness acknowledges that when we learn, we enter mystery. The learning will be larger than we are—we cannot know beforehand how we (or our clients) will grow through this process. Sacredness means that this process is bigger than our current state of knowledge.

Instilling sacredness is not about props, prayer, or religious ceremony. It's simply an intention that we are entering, and open to, mystery. How wonderful it is that teaching and learning involve sacred mystery. We can create rich, deep, meaningful educational settings or we cannot create them. Which would you prefer?

LEARNING AS A WAY OF TEACHING

WHEN I EMBARK on something new that involves teaching, facilitating, coaching, or presenting material, I always view it as a learning experiment. It takes the pressure off. An experiment means that it's uncertain. I'm testing things, trying things out, and using feedback to modify my procedures. Since it's an experiment, I don't have all the answers stored up inside me. It's helpful for me to tell people that it's an experiment—this gets them engaged in a more playful, experimental mode, as well. In *Getting Messy*, I use the word *learning* to emphasize what I believe our true role is when we teach, instruct, coach, or facilitate others. You can substitute the words *explore* or *experiment* for "learn," if you like. I admit these words are a little sexier. I'm just partial to the word learning. I believe it hasn't been given its due.

A great teacher *is* a revolutionary of sorts. Learning, by its very nature, moves us beyond established systems of knowledge and ways of doing things. Learning takes us outside of the box and beyond our comfort zones. A great teacher, whether operating in a formal capacity or an informal one, invites us to inquire and explore beyond what we currently know. As Palmer wrote, "The true work of the mind is to reconnect us with that which would otherwise be out of reach." And that's exactly what teachers do—they connect us with those things that would otherwise be out of reach.

Strong learners have a well-developed capacity to think "critically," which means the ability to question assumptions, embrace ambiguity, and hold multiple perspectives. Yet in many professional environments we don't often exercise these skills, as we usually assume that there is only one right way. For example, "active learning" has been a hot topic in educational circles. Its proponents argue that learning is, or should be, an *active* experience. That sounds good, but when active learning becomes a decree for all teaching situations it stifles the creativity and fluidity that is necessary for learning.

In *The Courage to Teach,* Palmer presents a humorous example of an angry chemistry professor at a large university who proclaims that he will *not* use role-playing in his classroom. Our fancy methods can be a wonderful thing, but they do not necessarily work in *all* situations. Despite good intentions, it's not helpful to latch onto methods without critically thinking about what we are doing. The belief that there is only one right way has led us to unimaginative and boring presentations, seminars, meetings, and so on.

If we're working in a teaching capacity as presenter or group leader, we need strong, well-developed capacities for critical thought, including the capacity to question, explore options, and be open to what works best given the situation at hand. If we believe we must follow some sort of system composed of rules, strategies, and techniques, we have no freedom to create something new. We have positioned ourselves with something fixed, not something fluid and flexible that supports growth. Life is fluid. Learning is fluid. Our methods need to be fluid as well.

Our techniques are often superfluous anyway. It's the *particulars* that matter—*this client*, *this topic*, and *this situation*. In management literature, this is called "contingency theory"— methods are contingent upon the unique situation in front of you. Many of our learned procedures are useless when we are face to face with a particular situation. If we work with other people in a professional capacity, we must be learners. We must be willing to not know.

Being a learner helps immensely when we're confronted with situations we're not prepared for. A corporate trainer walked into the room where he was supposed to lead a seminar and discovered that he didn't have any of his requested supplies. He eventually acquired the needed materials, but during that first session he had to quickly improvise a solution for entertaining 20 bored executives. Many years ago I led a large discussion group for older adults. It was all very pleasant, and then all of a sudden a woman stood up and shockingly started screaming at a man on the other side of the room. I'm sure you all have your own stories to relay, but the point is that you can't prepare for every situation that will come up. The group is bigger than you are. You don't have absolute control.

What can we do in the face of the unknown? We can be learners. We can investigate what is before us: *What is this situation asking of me? What, or who, do I need to pay attention to right now? What do I need to learn here? What lesson may be here for the entire group?* By diving underneath our systems and strategies to the level that actually holds growth and learning, we find renewed inspiration.

Some very basic learning principles are what I took with me when I walked into my first formal teaching situation. These principles and others are described throughout this book:

- paying attention
- being curious
- connecting to what feels true for me
- staying open to new possibilities
- allowing what wants to emerge
- using feedback to alter course

I have also discovered that I need to reach under the day's written agenda to the level that inspires and supports *my* learning, because my own growth and creativity are the only things that will ultimately renew me.

Being a strong learner is necessary for success in any occupation. I once heard an interview of a man who runs a program for at-risk youth. It became clear during the course of the interview what an impressive role model he was for these kids. He was an impressive role model not because of his expertise or charm, but because of his humility. He admitted that he was simply *learning* how to be a mentor to these youth; he didn't have all the answers; and furthermore, he didn't have all the answers in his new role of father either. With both pride and humility in his voice he said, "I'm a father. I'm not a great father, but I'm *learning* how to be a great father."

His words were echoed recently by President Barack Obama, who had this to say about fatherhood: "I've been far from perfect. But in the end it's not about being perfect. It's not always about succeeding. It's about always trying. And that's something everybody can do."

WHO THIS BOOK IS FOR

*G**ETTING MESSY* addresses teaching and learning in a broad array of settings. As should be evident by now, teaching and learning cut across a wide number of domains—from high-level corporate seminars to local community events. This book may be most helpful for those of you who work with adults in retreat centers, corporations, hospitals, senior centers, government, non-profit agencies, community colleges, universities, professional schools, and continuing education programs. The term *teacher* is meant to be broadly defined— trainers, consultants, mentors, coaches, parents, managers, workshop leaders, and group facilitators all work with people in a teaching capacity. Anyone who is responsible in some way for another person's experience is a teacher.

The term *learning* is also meant to be broadly defined, since we learn in a variety of ways and environments throughout our daily life. I've tried to present a broad range of examples from professional environments. Whatever example is being provided, please apply it to your own situation.

Finally, the words *student* and *client* will be used interchangeably in this book to refer to the participants in your workshops, your colleagues, your patients, the people you direct or manage, or whomever you work with in a teaching capacity. The terms students, clients, colleagues, and participants are meant to be used reciprocally. I often use the term "group" in this book to refer to the participants in your teaching situation. If you are a coach or mentor, you can assume that "group" in this case refers to you and your client.

There are very few situations in today's world in which we're not required to learn or teach information to others. And more and more, modern-day jobs require creativity and flexibility. This book will help you find inspiration when you need it, learn how to "flow" better in chaotic environments, and tap the incredible resources contained within a group.

Getting Messy is intended to be an inspiration and a friend, a place you can turn to for wisdom when problems occur and for renewed energy when you find yourself drained of ideas. It is offered with deep appreciation to those of you who spend your lives helping people learn.

HOW TO USE THIS BOOK

THIS BOOK presents a framework and some principles that will assist you in developing a learning perspective when you teach or work with other people. It is my hope that you will use this book to instigate a deeper inquiry into the heart of your work: *Who are you when you teach? What are you offering*

your students (clients, participants)? How can your work be renew-
ing to you? How can this work help you grow?

As a framework for this learning process, I would like
to tell you about a method of research in the social sciences
called *Organic Inquiry.* Initially developed in the 1990s, it is a
feminist approach to scholastic research that is exploratory
and discovery-oriented. It arose because of frustration with
traditional research methods that view the scientist as totally
removed from what he or she is studying. Organic Inquiry is
especially well suited for investigating elusive topics and for
fostering insights about topics that have had a profound personal effect on the inquirer. For example, a scholar may be
studying rape as a topic of research, yet also have a deeply
personal connection with this topic. These personal associations necessarily influence the research study, yet are viewed
as unimportant by traditional methods. Organic Inquiry
acknowledges and allows personal associations and incorporates them into the research data.

What I realized upon encountering it, however, is that
Organic Inquiry is not limited to collecting research data; it
also gives us a model for how humans learn in everyday life.
After all, research is really a process of structured learning.
When scholars decide to study something, they are beginning
an investigative process, one where they wish to understand
something new and unfamiliar.

The aim in Organic Inquiry is not to present data that is
objective and generalized, as all other research methods aim to
do. Rather, the aim is to present the data and analysis in such
a way that the individual reader may interact with it and be
transformed by it. In other words, the research process itself is
viewed as transformational. In order for this transformation to
occur, you first create a "container" for learning—something

the authors call *sacred space*. (See Clements & colleagues' *Organic Inquiry: If Research Were Sacred*.)

Virginia Woolf, in *A Room of One's Own*, reminded us of the need for our own sanctuary in order to write or create. The same is true for learning. While Woolf was speaking of a physical room, we can view her suggestion metaphorically as well. When we create *room* for ourselves, we allow stillness and silence so that we can hear our own thoughts and observations. One of the first things we need to do as learners is intentionally create room for learning. This space for learning is not unbounded. It has edges, creating a container for our pursuit. When you read this book, you will have your own organic inquiry. Whatever thoughts, ideas, and feelings arise for you are important; they are part of your individual journey with this material.

In the *Reflection* section that follows this chapter I offer some suggestions for how to create learning space. One important way to create space is to dedicate a journal or notebook to the learning process. My journal in this case was titled, *An Organic Inquiry about Organic Inquiry*. During the course of reading about Organic Inquiry, I noted what came up for me with regard to the topic—any emotions or reactions I had to reading the material, dreams, synchronistic events and chance phone calls, in addition to all of my thoughts, research, and reflections. What came up for me was my own personal "research data" into Organic Inquiry.

I like the use of the term sacred, because defining this process as sacred makes us notice and value what does come up, rather than dismissing it as unimportant. We can meet each moment with the expectation that our environment may yield messages that are addressed to us personally. Dreams, intuitions, synchronistic meetings, random thoughts, feelings—this everyday material is our source of learning and may be directly speaking to our current questions. If we view the occurrences of our everyday life as sacred, we are more likely to pay attention to them.

Organic Inquiry presents us with a very different way of reading a book. Typically, our learning model has been one of information-processing. We read. We digest. We spit out. There is very little "chewing," i.e., letting the material seep in and "work" us. The kind of learning that we will be doing here is holistic, not purely cognitive. If it were solely cognitive, I would present my material and you would swallow it. However, in our Organic Inquiry we're required to go deeper into the learning process. We're going to chew a little—not only tasting our "food," but differentiating the flavors, allowing our own insights to surface. The point here is not to give answers, but rather to help you connect with your own voice.

Learning, especially in adulthood, is driven by our passions, interests, and questions. It's an internal process—we *choose* what we wish to learn. Our inner voice is the central directing element, shifting us in certain directions and away from others. In Chapter Two we investigate learning as a process of discovering what we love, discernment, critical thinking, and trusting ourselves.

In Chapter Three we create *internal* space for learning, exploring the arena of imagination. Imaginal space presents us with new possibilities. We are beginning to move beyond what we currently know, into what we don't know; we are making new connections.

In Chapter Four we create *external* space for learning, developing a proper appreciation of structure. Structure is what allows space for our possibilities to sprout. It is partly *physical*, created by four walls and the arrangement of chairs. It's partly created by having adequate *time* to allow learning to occur and freedom from distractions. It's partly *conceptual*, created by how we frame the topic for learning. And it's partly created by our *intentions* and *ground rules*, having guidelines that create opportunities for real dialogue.

In Chapter Five we are learners, immersing ourselves in a relationship with something that's bigger than we are. What does it mean to be *learners* when we facilitate a group or coach a client? We investigate the necessity of stepping out of the role, becoming empty, meeting clients as equals, paying attention, speaking our truth, cultivating connections, learning from diversity, and allowing what wants to emerge.

And in Chapter Six we dive into the most difficult situations that many of us experience at one point or another. We learn about third space and what it means to teach from that place. We are true learners, critically reflecting on our challenges and growing from them.

And because we don't just learn by taking in information, at the end of each chapter are a series of suggested reflective questions and activities, grouped into five sections: *Creating Space, Renewing Inspiration, Planting Seeds, Tending the Field,* and *Digging Deeper.* Just as it sounds, *Creating Space* is meant to help you create space for learning in your teaching work. Learning space has both internal and external components. Your commitment and openness create internal learning space. External learning space is created by the arrangements you make to foster learning in your life. *Renewing Inspiration* and *Planting Seeds* will help you develop new possibilities for your work. The questions and exercises in *Tending the Field* will help you process the information you will be receiving.

Finally, in *Digging Deeper* I present ways for you to develop a deeper understanding of a particular issue or situation. These exercises will also help you begin to open up your imagination to a wider range of possibilities for your work. We explore guided visualizations, sentence completion exercises, collage, intuitive insight, art and poetry, and dialoguing through fairy tales and other writing methods. Since problems can't be solved at the level at which they were created, we have to go beyond the level of the problem to a place of higher vision, in order to see the solution. The exercises in *Digging Deeper* are intended to help you enter that greater place of understanding.

This book is meant to be a place where you can have a provocative conversation—with the material, with new ideas, and with yourself. I hope this book refreshes and renews you, giving you a sense of expanded possibility and the means to make those possibilities a reality. I encourage you to see where you can move outside the lines. I invite you to get messy.

REFLECTING
ON YOUR EXPERIENCE

Creating Space . . .

Buy a journal specifically dedicated to learning about your teaching work.

> Title it anything you wish. This journal forms a container where your ideas, insights, inspirations, and thoughts can emerge. It's a place where you can process what comes up for you and keep track of your plans and visions. This journal is a place you have set aside for listening to your Self.

Make an intention to find your own voice in your work.

> An internal commitment to learn helps to create a strong learning space. Your commitment will guide you as you step out into new experiences. Commitment is necessary because we don't live in a world where interior space is seen or acknowledged.

Write your intention in your journal.

> *"I, Carla Smith, commit to learning what I need to learn in order to be a great presenter." Or "I, Bill Jones, commit to opening up and exploring my own creativity in my work and in my life." Write down any other thoughts and intentions that seem relevant.*

Renewing Inspiration . . .

Quick… think "school." Say the word "school" to yourself and write down what immediately comes to mind.

Write down the standard, accepted definition of the word "teacher."

Next, write down the opposite of the above definition.

Finally, write down your own unique definition for "teacher."

Here are some of my definitions:

> *A teacher is someone who brings fresh possibility and ideas, so people are inspired to learn.*

> *A teacher is someone who nourishes a person's roots so they can grow. A teacher has rich soil.*

> *A teacher creates space for learning.*

Your definition of a teacher may be very different from what is considered normal.

Does your own definition serve you and your work? How so?

Given your definition of a teacher, does your current environment allow you to "be" this teacher?

Given your definition, what is your ideal type of work? What is your ideal working environment?

Planting Seeds . . .

Write down thoughts, reflections, dreams, and synchronistic events as they occur.

Now that you have formed your intention and created a container, whatever comes up in your everyday life that seems to be related to your inquiry is all part of the process. In addition to your thoughts and reflections, note any synchronistic meetings or phone calls, unusual dreams, and the reactions and emotions that occur for you as you read this book. Keep lists of things that strike you as funny or silly, and the things that make you angry are also important messages. Write down notes from pertinent books you come across, ideas from interesting lectures and workshops, and so on. The things that speak to you are part of your unique learning journey.

Tending The Field ...

Schedule time with yourself.

> Our everyday lives are usually comprised of activities that offer no refuge for the self at all. Devote 20 minutes each week to reflect on what has meaning for you in your work and to contemplate your next areas of growth. You can view the process as one of creating a protected container to honor your learning.
>
> Make a list of five things you can do to give yourself some quiet, reflective time. For example, going to the beach or listening to music are things that may give you time to process and allow your subconscious mind to provide you with new insights...

1.

2.

3.

4.

5.

Digging Deeper . . .

Develop an initial vision for your work.

Seat yourself in a comfortable position and close your eyes. For a few moments, simply get comfortable and pay attention to your breathing. Then ask yourself for a metaphorical image that portrays a vision for your work. Spend some time with your image; let it tell you whatever it has to share. After you're finished, list whatever insights are suggested from the image. Don't try to make sense of them given your current work situation, just list as many qualities from the image as you can.

The image that I often get is that of a farmer. In one hand, he has a pail full of seeds, and in the other, a pail full of water. Here are possibilities that I get from this image: nourishment (the pail of water), being a good steward (the farmer), potential (the pail of seeds), patience (the seeds need to be planted and don't grow all at once), care (the farmer cares about his work), and humility (the farmer is wearing old coveralls.)

CHAPTER TWO

Connecting to Inner Wisdom

The leader who is centered and grounded can work with erratic people and critical group situations without harm. Being centered means having the ability to recover one's balance, even in the midst of action. A centered person is not subject to passing whims or sudden excitements. Being grounded means being down-to-earth, having gravity or weight. I know where I stand, and I know what I stand for; that is ground. The centered and grounded leader has stability and a sense of self.

— JOHN HEIDER, *THE TAO OF LEADERSHIP*

2

EXPRESSING YOUR OWN IMAGE

OVER THE COURSE of our lives, most of us spend many, many hours in classrooms and training rooms, involved in what is commonly called a "learning" process. *Getting Messy* presents a somewhat different view of learning. Whether we are young or old, whether we are sitting in a classroom or not, learning can rarely be forced upon us. We may temporarily memorize something to pass a test, but then we will promptly forget it. When we actually *learn* something, it is a freewill choice. Our inner curiosities, questions, and interests are what are *really* directing our inquiry. In this chapter we look at learning in more detail, a process that involves discovering what we love, discerning what speaks to us, thinking critically, and trusting our own insights.

Perhaps because we've so often viewed learners as passive, subject to the whims and demands of someone else, being a learner is not viewed as hip in today's world. Think of the terms we use for learners: "neophyte," "wet behind the ears," "plebe," "a beginner." Our goal is always to become skilled and knowledgeable—to lose our beginner status so we can gain in social standing and prestige.

In truth, learning is a creative process. What an artist does is take in impressions of the world around him. He then processes those impressions and offers back something unique—a unique perspective or expression. The sound of a babbling brook may inspire a piece of music, crowds on the subway may inspire a textile artist, the scent of homemade bread may inspire a novel. This unique expression is what we were all meant to do.

As learners, the material we are working with is *ideas* and *information* rather than sensory input, but we are still taking in impressions and processing those impressions. We take in information from the world, filter it through our own unique lens, and offer back a distinct point of view that expresses, in some way, who we are. This is what we do when we learn and we are all naturally creative in this way. For example, let's say you have room of 20 people who have all read the same set of standard materials. When you ask the group for their responses to this material, you will likely get 20 different interpretations. How a person reads and interprets something is necessarily going to be unique. That's the beauty of learning.

Over seven centuries ago, Dante Alighieri claimed that we are driven by the desire to express our own image:

> For in every action, whether caused by necessity or free will, the main intention of the agent is to express his own image; thus it is that every doer, whenever he does, enjoys the doing; because everything that is desires to be, and in action the

doer unfolds his being, enjoyment naturally follows, for a thing desired always brings delight...
Therefore, nothing acts without making itself
manifest. (The translation for this quote was
found in a book by Mihaly Csikszentmihalyi and
Eugene Halton, *The Meaning of Things.*)

In modern times, we witness the innate desire to express
and "unfold" in the dramatic success of high school creative arts programs and youth-oriented poetry slams.
Interestingly, those programs spur students on to further
academic learning, and not necessarily in the arts. By being
able to see the core of their own potential, young people are
naturally driven to learn more in a variety of fields, because
they've connected with that deeper part of themselves that
wants to express itself—that part that wants to learn.

One of my favorite quotes about learning is from Donald
Oliver, who writes in *Education and Community,* "Knowledge, trea-
sured as the gift of education, is really only useful as a catalyst
for the active use of the student's creativity. Not used for this
purpose, knowledge simply amounts to inert ideas." Learning
is a process where we become more of ourselves, shedding what
doesn't fit and moving into what does.

DISCOVERING WHAT YOU LOVE

PSYCHOLOGISTS SAY that two things motivate human beings:
love and fear. In the field of teaching and learning, the terms
we use are intrinsic and extrinsic motivation. When we're

extrinsically motivated, we're pushed to do something because we'll be rewarded for it (or risk punishment if we don't). When we're intrinsically motivated, on the other hand, we do something because we want to do it. We need no external incentives. As previously discussed, learning in adulthood is nearly always intrinsically motivated because it's not possible to force someone to learn something against their will. It may be possible to memorize something for a short period of time, but this is much different than the deeper path of learning about something. Therefore, to be learners in the world, we need to know what we are interested in. We need to discover what we love.

Love is not anti-intellectual. In fact, it's quite the opposite—our loves and passions *inspire* our intellects. "People cannot learn what they do not love," Johann Wolfgang von Goethe told us. The most effective people in any occupation are those who love their work, and the most effective teachers are those who can share that passion with others. Margaret Rosenheim, voted Teacher of the Year at the University of Chicago, said, "Teaching is a matter of love—the love you have for your own material and the love you feel about imparting its importance." If love—for learning, your clients, your field—is driving your teaching work, you'll be effective. And if your heart isn't present, your clients will know. Mozart wrote, "Neither a lofty intelligence nor imagination nor both together go to the making of genius. Love, love, love—that is the soul of genius."

You can see the truth of Mozart's statement in the architectural designs of Temple Grandin. Grandin is a scholar who has designed several new facilities for livestock. (Her story is told in her book, *Thinking in Pictures*.) She was concerned about the animals and wanted to reduce their level of anxiety. In order to help the animals feel safer and more comforted, she made the walls of the transport area high and curved to give the animals a feeling of being held. Her designs for curved chutes and other innovations have won several international awards. Grandin's love and compassion sparked her genius. No one else cared enough to go to the trouble of thinking through the problem and coming up with something brilliant. Grandin cared.

While reading *Getting Messy*, listen to what your heart has to say. Our hearts are what move us into action. Our loves are what sustain us through difficult days. Trying to do things to please others doesn't work. Staying on your own path is ultimately the only path you can take. What places or activities inspire you? You probably have inklings about what your unique treats are—browsing a bookstore, looking through art books, taking a hike, listening to music while you run on the beach, conversing with someone knowledgeable, attending a lecture, or spending time reflecting and writing.

Many generative experiences involve the senses, not only our visual capacities, but also tasting, touching, hearing, smelling. You might want to explore poetry, cooking, music, or dance. See what activities take you into creative territory where new thoughts arise. There are no "shoulds" here. Maybe dance inspires your creativity, but poetry leaves you cold. Alternatively, maybe reading others' poetry does nothing for you, but writing your own ignites your creative flames. Find out what inspires you and schedule time to soak in that energy. This is your time to explore.

To discover what you love, you need to *let the world in*—a world that's rich in possibilities. We can presume that everything is alive and speaking to us, as psychologist James Hillman writes in a wonderful passage from *The Soul's Code:*

> The world is made less of nouns than of verbs. It does not consist merely in objects and things; it is filled with useful, playful, and intriguing opportunities. The oriole doesn't see a branch, but an occasion for perching; the cat doesn't see a thing we call an empty box, it sees safe hiding for peering. The bear doesn't smell honeycomb, but the opportunity for delicious feeding. The world is buzzing and blooming with information, which is always available and never absent.

Hillman invites us to move out of our "psychological" homes—the home of our parents—and take a leap out into the home of the world. There we find our inspirations. We let the world in and discover what moves our hearts.

The path of a butterfly beautifully illustrates this somewhat non-linear, non-rational process. The butterfly flits around, landing on this flower, then that one. The prettiest flower is the one that catches its eye, and it moves on when it is ready—to the next thing it finds delightful. The butterfly is following its natural interests, and it's interesting to note: *The things that it's attracted to are good for it.* The butterfly doesn't have a five-year plan, it simply keeps moving to the next attractive thing. Perhaps this sounds narcissistic or hedonistic, but many of us have lost the ability to follow our passions. We've let other things get in the way until we no longer have an authentic connection to what speaks to us.

For example, away on a retreat, you might walk into the dining hall and see several different tables of people who are in your seminar or workshop. Rather than go to the closest table, or the safest table, it would serve your learning to go to the table to which you are most *attracted*. Perhaps you are attracted to a table where someone who said something challenging is sitting, or perhaps a particular group simply looks interesting to you. It might not be a logical reason. Your mind, on the other hand, might be telling you to choose the table with the seminar leader so you can win some points or the table of people who are in your line of work so you can do some networking. If you feel moved to join a "non-rational" table, that is the one you need to sit at. Learning is not always linear or logical. Sometimes it is. Often it is not. We learn by stepping out, noticing what attracts our attention, and following and trusting our instincts.

When we're in touch with our own inspirations and passions, we will more profoundly reach our clients and students. We will be able to tap their internal motivators because we have tapped our own. What do you find beautiful about your subject or line of work? What inspires you? What fascinates you? If you don't see it, the participants in your workshops or classes surely won't. The fire for learning begins with the teacher, or as an Italian proverb states, "Who shall kindle others must himself glow."

DISCERNMENT

HOW DO WE FIGURE out where our passions lie? By developing skills of noticing and perceiving. We need the ability to connect with our inner selves and notice what is occurring for us. We need to be able to notice where *our own* truth lies. This skill is necessary in any learning process because learning requires that we traverse new terrain. When we traverse new terrain, we need a guide and the guide is within ourselves. The faculties that guide us and help us make choices are our own natural reactions.

I hear many presenters say what a shock it is the first time they make some off-the-cuff remark and they see the participants in their seminar dutifully writing it down. Many people come ready to swallow whatever you have to say. But other people are on the other end of the spectrum: They've already decided not to listen to you. People in the first group are too open, the second group too closed. Both of these positions are common and neither helps us learn in any creative way. When we are too closed, we are obviously not receptive to learning. But when we're too open, we're not discriminatory enough. We take in too much and then we inevitably come to a point where we have to shut down.

I would like to suggest a third way: A stance of openness and willingness to take in information, guidance, or advice, without swallowing it whole. By developing the ability to decipher what speaks to us, we avoid becoming carbon copies of others. This does not mean shutting out the world. It means having confidence in our own ability to learn in a way that is healthy for us. Clearly, with the wealth of information and opportunities that are available, we need our reasoning and discernment abilities to be plugged in and operational.

In addition to the overwhelming quantity of information in this world, the other reason that we need the ability to discern is because there is no information that's unbiased and value-free. Knowledge has typically been viewed as a neutral entity, something that is out there in the world that we can "gain." All we have to do is read, study, and memorize and we will "know" it.

But even scientifically-controlled research studies are not objective. Many scientists today are disclosing that their research is not, and will never be, value-free. Scientists hold a point of view and these views influence both the data itself (what data is collected, how it is collected), as well as the interpretation of the results. I spent years doing quantitative research studies and I quickly discovered that depending upon what variables I used in my equations, I would get dramatically different findings. Since the researcher is deciding what variables to use, quantitative research is clearly the result of his or her worldview. The researcher determines what findings are seen as legitimate and has the sole power to dismiss others as inconclusive. The same is true, of course, for qualitative research. There is no such thing as thoroughly objective knowledge.

No one is a neutral observer of the world. Research reports, journal articles, and academic textbooks all present a particular point of view. Further, all fields hold differences in approach, technique, and philosophy. No matter what sort of teaching you do, there is no way you can provide thoroughly impartial information to your clients or students. The questions that you pose are the result of how you look at the world—your personal experiences, values, and beliefs. No matter how neutral you wish to be, the information you present will always be slanted in some way.

All this has one serious consequence: The false assumption that knowledge is impartial (value-free) leads directly to a lack of critical thought. The reason? When we presume that information is unbiased, there is no reason not to swallow it wholesale. Isn't that right? On the other hand, if we know that information is subjective (as all information is), we must necessarily regard it more carefully and thoughtfully.

Skilled learners have a built-in filtering process, which partly involves the capacity to notice what speaks to them. Learning happens when we connect with a topic in a way that holds meaning for us. Some scholars have argued that knowledge *only* exists in us when it's meaningful in our lives, and I am sure that this is true for adults. It's precisely the subjectivity of knowledge that gives it validity.

Think of the opposite situation—information that is removed from the learner's subjective experience. (Information that is *not* meaningful to one's life.) This situation gives us an image of the teacher as someone who is "molding" and "directing" the minds of his or her students. Clearly, when information is not meaningful to us, being required to learn it is dehumanizing. We become mere instruments or tools of the information, holding no sense of responsibility for what we've learned. (For more on this, see Zvi Lamm's chapter in *Curriculum: An Introduction to the Field*.)

On the other hand, when we make a *choice* to learn something, we naturally feel a sense of responsibility and ownership toward it. In *Art and Fear*, David Bayles and Ted Orland were addressing artists, but their words apply to all of us: "The only work really worth doing—the only work you *can* do convincingly—is the work that focuses on the things you care about. To not focus on those issues is to deny the constants in your life."

CRITICAL THINKING

PEOPLE OFTEN CONFUSE critical thinking with finding things to disagree with. The word "critical" gets in our way here, perhaps. Most of us believe critical thinking involves looking outward, trying to find some little piece to criticize or dispute. I will never forget the endless hours of "critical thinking" we did in my graduate school classes. We nearly always missed the meat of a lively conversation because we were busy picking apart the minutia. When we read a research study, we grasped onto the minute details because we could easily analyze and dispute them. We rarely dived into the heart of a topic.

In his book *Jupiter's Rings*, Howard Schechter writes that the critical process that we learn at home and in school later becomes a habit: "...we become addicted to the negative energy bundled into it in the same way people become addicted to gossip. But looking for defects in others or their opinions does not serve us. It produces division and acrimony." Critical thinking has nothing to do with one-upmanship, intellectual jousting matches, or verbally destroying other people's work.

So let's enlarge our standard view of critical thinking to embrace a more holistic perspective, one that serves us better. In my view, critical thinking is the ability to look under the surface of what is being said and discussed. And it involves examining our own lenses and perspectives through which we are thinking and responding. Critical thinking is about looking *deeper*. A later exercise will offer a detailed set of queries, but for now, here are some sample questions to get you started:

- What are the larger ramifications of this discussion?
- What are the motivations and belief systems that underlie the author or speaker's opinions and the way he (or she) frames and discusses issues?
- What are the motivations and belief systems that underlie my own opinions? Through what lens am *I* viewing the world?

- If I'm having a strong reaction, such as anger or frustration, to a particular book, set of ideas, or person, why might I be having this reaction? What "truth" is underneath my emotional reaction?
- What two or three main ideas do I get out of this piece of writing, lecture, or conversation? What ideas here stimulate and inspire me?
- Do I feel comfortable in this learning situation? Why or why not? Am I gaining something from this experience?
- Is this conversation making me feel invigorated or energized? Or is it making me feel sluggish? Why might this be?

We can see then that "critical" does not mean "criticize." Rather, we can define "critical" as being serious. We are fully committed to serious reflection on this matter. We are serious in our attempt to fully listen, take in, and examine. We are committed to waking up and seeing more clearly. We are going to take a good hard look, set aside as many preconceptions and belief systems and opinions as we can, and develop an understanding about something that feels more accurate. We are going to look under the surface.

Critical thinking is more about depth than breadth. Critical thinkers look under issues and state truths that haven't been spoken. Most importantly, critical thinkers look within and uncover the basis of their *own* thoughts, ideas, and feelings. Learning is an internal process.

Connecting to your self involves the ability to decipher and make choices based on both your cognitive capacities and an intuitive, felt sense of rightness or wrongness. When you connect to your self in critical thinking, you are able to discern how you feel about whatever is happening in your environment.

This requires the capacity to connect with your emotions and use them as the basis of your inquiry. As the British writer and philosopher A.R. Orage once said, "A man can only think as deeply as he feels." With the ability to connect to your sensory and emotional spheres, you can scan information and pull out what's useful to you, disregarding what is not.

The skill of discernment requires our wholeness. In other words, it not only requires our minds but also our hearts, as the character of Sherlock Holmes discovers in Laurie King's novel, *A Letter of Mary*. In the novel, Sherlock writes a letter to a friend:

> My dear Russell. Many years ago, in my foolish youth...I was quite convinced that strong emotion interfered with rational thought, like grit in a sensitive instrument. I believed the heart to be a treacherous organ that served only to cloud the mind, and now...now I find myself in the disturbing position of having my mind at odds with—with the rest of me. Once I would have automatically followed the dictates of my reasoning mind. However, I begin to suspect that—and I shall say this quietly—that I was wrong, that there may be times when the heart sees something which the mind does not. Perhaps what we call the heart is simply a more efficient means of evaluating data. Perhaps I mistrust it because I cannot see the mechanism working.

Our hearts are often more useful than our minds when we need to make genuine discriminations. Many writers and scholars have argued that the ability to discriminate comes from the wisdom of the heart. For example, Sigmund Freud told us, "In the small matters trust the mind; in the large ones the heart." And Charles Dickens wrote, "A loving heart is the truest wisdom."

So what exactly is this distinction between head and heart? I would say that accessing the heart's wisdom offers us a greater level of awareness and comprehension. If we are merely processing information from the mind, our projections, preconceived ideas, and attitudes easily get in our way, clouding our vision. Our cognitive minds often block learning from happening by developing and storing intricate sets of beliefs over time. Once these belief systems become solid, they shut down any information that might take us beyond them. I am sure you've met people who won't associate with others who hold different religious beliefs or political views. The more rigid our views are, the more out of touch with reality we become. Most of us humans feel we need to live by our belief systems in order to feel secure in the world. But with this security comes a lack of openness to what the world has to offer. In his book, *Think on These Things*, J. Krishnamurti writes,

> If you hold firmly to some set of beliefs or other, you look at everything through that particular prejudice or tradition, you don't have any contact with reality...[But] if you have no prejudice, no bias, if you are open, then everything around you becomes extraordinarily interesting, tremendously alive.

How do you know that you are processing something from your heart and not your head? First, notice how your body feels. When you speak something that is deeply true for you,

you can often feel it in your body—a shiver, a wave of emo-tion, a feeling of deep calm. Second, if you are feeling edgy, angry, resentful, frustrated, and so on, you are probably not in your heart. When the heart processes information, there is a feeling of calmness and peace. Finally, the heart feels love and compassion. If you are in a situation where you feel some compassion—for yourself, the assignment you are working on, the seminar leader who is speaking at the front of the room, the material you are going to present to your client tomorrow—this is your heart speaking.

We can critically reflect on three levels. The first level is the individual level of thoughts, feelings, and beliefs. On this level we are alone, viewing a newscast, reading a book, or reflecting on a lecture we've just heard. Critical reflection would involve attend-ing to our reactions, particularly if we feel angry or annoyed with the author or lecturer. In this instance, critical reflection would not mean simply coming up with some quick, easy answer such as, "The author is too idealistic." Perhaps he *is* idealistic, but if you are getting an emotional charge (feeling frustrated, annoyed, resentful) from reading the book or listening to the lecture, there is something there for you to uncover and learn about yourself. Otherwise, you wouldn't feel angry or annoyed.

Critical reflection can also occur when you are with a client or colleague. What do you notice with this other per-son? Do you feel distant? If so, what is causing the feeling of disconnection? Are you feeling uncomfortable, or do you feel secure and safe? After you leave his or her presence, do you feel happy? Light? Free? Or do you feel heavy, gloomy, or anxious? Critical thinking includes the ability to sense when someone is speaking authentically and when someone is not. Again, this ability comes not from our minds or a textbook, but from our hearts and bodies.

Finally, critical reflection occurs on the group level as well. You might ask yourself: What is going on in this group? What seems to be an underlying dynamic here? Who is holding power in this group and who is not? Is this group balanced and working well, or is it unbalanced? Do I feel happy and content here or am I uncomfortable? What do I need to do to feel more comfortable? Am I holding back from saying something that really needs to be said?

The term critical thinking is often tossed around casually, but it's not a casual or a simple concept. It takes an ongoing commitment to learning because it's difficult to continue to notice what is coming up for us and pay attention to it. Critical thinking takes effort and requires that we view our own thoughts and feelings as important and worth paying attention to. We're not looking outward at the externals so much as examining our *own* internal process—our feelings, thoughts, and reactions.

With critical thinking, we can find our way through the plethora of opinions and belief systems that make up modern society. We can take in information, but without swallowing it whole. We can spend more time chewing.

Earlier in the chapter I offered a few questions that would invoke critical thinking. Picking up from where we left off, here is a complete list of critically reflective questions:

Examples of critically reflective questions for encountering new information in the form of lectures or books include:

- How does this material inspire my own thoughts?
- What is the broader social context of this issue?

- What are other options or alternatives?
- What analogies or associations can I make? (i.e., what is this material like?) Is there a metaphor that will deepen my understanding of this topic?
- Am I feeling any strong emotions (anger, confusion, etc.) when I read this book or listen to this lecturer? What might be the source of this feeling?
- What is this person (author, lecturer, etc.) not seeing?
- Is this person's assertion always true?
- What assumptions and belief systems frame this person's argument?
- What assumptions and belief systems frame my *own* opinion?

I often use an exercise called Sentence Completions in order to access deeper beliefs and unconscious attitudes. To do a sentence completion, write down the sentence stem that is given and then finish the sentence with whatever words come to you. It's important to do these quickly, without thinking. Even if the answers seem strange or unusual, write them down. The following are some you might try. Choose one and repeat it five or six times until you get an answer that surprises you.

- The way I can best engage with this material is…
- What is missing for me with this material is…
- What this material is offering me is…

Examples of critically reflective questions when you are speaking with someone include:

- Do I feel open in this conversation? If so, why?
- Are new thoughts being stimulated?
- Do I feel uncomfortable? If so, why?
- What are we not seeing? What is missing in this discussion?

Sentence completions:

- The reason I feel uncomfortable with this person is…
- The reason I like to speak with this person is…
- The way I can improve my communication with this person is…
- The thing that I need to say in this conversation is…

Examples of critically reflective questions you can use in a group situation include:

- Do I feel comfortable or uncomfortable here?
- What body sensations or thoughts are giving me these impressions?
- What do I need to do to take care of myself in this situation?
- How can this group work better?
- How can this group work better for *me*?
- Is there something in this group that is not being said?

Sentence completions:

- The way I can take care of myself in this situation right now is…
- The way this group can work better is…
- The reason I feel uncomfortable in this group is…
- The reason I feel comfortable in this group is…

Experiment with whatever questions above seem most appropriate to the situation. See if you can begin to develop more critically reflective abilities in a range of everyday situations.

TRUSTING YOURSELF

AN ACQUAINTANCE recently shared with me that she was embarrassed that she'd never developed her own opinions while she was in school. When her teachers asked her to write a critique of a poem or piece of literature, she would go to the library and read what other people had written about the piece. She felt somewhat ashamed that she had never developed the capacity to come up with her own opinion, without reading what other people had written first.

My response to her was that in order to learn, we need something to chew on. Although learning is an internal process, it also requires that we *interact* with the world. We receive other people's writings and ideas, and let those ideas inspire our own thinking on the matter. Knowledge does not get uncovered, whole and complete, from within us. It takes an interaction with outside voices in order to uncover our own. Reading what others have to say and deciphering what ideas hit an inner truth chord helps develop our capacity for critical thought. We learn to take what fits and leave the rest. This is true in the creative process as well. Beethoven's early compositions were clearly influenced by his teacher, Haydn. In *Art and Fear*, Bayles and Orland write,

> Most early [artistic] work only hints at the themes and gestures that will—if the potential isn't squandered—emerge as the artist's characteristic signature in later, mature work. At the outset, however, chances are that whatever theme and technique attract you, someone has already experimented in the same

> direction...Finding your own work is a process
> of distilling from each those traces that ring
> true to your own spirit.

It's also true that my friend might have had her own response to the material, yet didn't allow herself time to explore it. How would she do that? She could start by noticing and recording her reactions to what she read: Did it make her bored, angry, sad, excited? These feelings are her ticket toward her own unique take on the material. She could then take those reactions and write from them.

It is true that it's easy to get into a pattern of letting experts think for us. Since there is someone who already knows the "answer," the rest of us don't have to bother to come up with our own. Over time, as we depend more on others to think for us, we start to distrust our own thoughts and ideas.

We have the most difficulty trusting ourselves when our response differs from everyone else's. This phenomenon has been documented in research studies. One study involved a group of people sitting around a table with flash cards. Nine of the ten participants were instructed beforehand to blatantly lie during the session. The tenth participant was clueless. On one task, the nine participants agreed that when comparing two images, the first image was larger than the second was. The tenth participant, the one who was not in on the lie, disagreed. To him, the second image was clearly larger than the first. The tenth participant couldn't understand what was going on. "Why are people saying things that aren't true?"

As the session went on and the nine others continued to put on a blank face to the charade, the tenth participant began to doubt himself. "Perhaps I'm wrong. Perhaps the first image IS larger than the first." He began to agree with the other participants, changing his responses to fit in with the group. Do you notice this in yourself? When everyone else in the room (or in your community) strongly shares the same view, it's more challenging to give a different response.

If you work in any sort of teaching capacity, you particularly need to develop a healthy trust in your own perceptions, because you are putting yourself in a position to be judged and evaluated. If you lead workshops, facilitate groups, present seminars, or hold community events, your attendees will decide for themselves whether they like what you are offering them. If you're a classroom teacher, the administration, fellow faculty, students, and parents may all have strong opinions. Teaching is an occupation that is fraught with ideology about what you should be doing, and you'll be regularly submitted to formal or informal judgments and evaluations of your work. It comes with the territory.

Further, depending on the sort of work you do, you may also receive advice from governmental agencies, non-profit organizations, research groups, and academic institutions. While their suggestions may be well meant, it's still overwhelming to negotiate and navigate all these points of view, which are often strong and deeply ingrained. Yet most us get little or no support for examining our own reactions and trusting our own intuitive voices.

Of course, we want to be open to advice and new ideas. But part of being learners is to know what speaks to us and what doesn't. The key to learning as adults is to develop trust in our own instincts, values, and understandings. If you are uncomfortable with a certain workshop, participant, situation, or organizational setting, you can trust that feeling. There is something there for you to look at and make a decision about. If you get some wacky idea of marching the seminar group down to the local café or bringing in a flamboyant guest speaker, follow up on that idea. Trust yourself. Have the courage to go against the conventional wisdom from time to time. There is no one right way to learn and thus there is no one right way to teach. We need to get in touch with our own innate wisdom. It's there.

In the last thirty years, numerous books have been written about accessing our intuition. (For one of the original bestsellers on intuition in everyday life, check out Frances Vaughan's 1978 book, *Awakening Intuition*.) The most important thing is not the methods we use to access intuition, but trusting the wisdom that we do get. Once you trust the messages that you are getting, you can call yourself intuitive.

Your way of working may have been greatly shaped by others, and your style may continue to shift and change over time as you take in new information. But advice is harmful when it moves you off your own center. Our own inner guidance needs to be the ultimate authority. The important point is to look within to what you are experiencing as valuable, instead of looking for what you are being told is valuable.

Learning requires a healthy sense of self. It requires the strong conviction that we *do* know, underneath all the layers of doubt and confusion. We *do* have an inner voice that knows. We can be open, willing, and able to hear others, and equally able to maintain our own center of integrity at the same time. We can choose to take in those things that support our own sense of rightness. This process is not often an intellectual one. It is visceral. It's on the feeling level. You will know as a felt sense whether some idea rings true or not. You will be able to feel when you are being shifted off your own center by other people's opinions.

DEVELOPING A VISION

Of ALL FIELDS, teaching and learning are probably the most fraught with beliefs, doctrines, convictions, and fancies. Clients, students, community members, your colleagues, the organization, and so on will all have opinions about what you should be doing and how you should be doing it. Because of this, having an underlying philosophy about what you are doing and why is invaluable. Without an intention motivating your work, it will be easy for you to be blown around in the wind, trying to please this person, then that, this client, this administrator, this colleague. A vision gives you and your work a strong foundation.

As you read this book and do the reflective exercises, your vision may begin to emerge. The Hebrew scholar Marc Gafni wrote, "In Hebrew, the word for 'salvation' translates as broad space. There's something salvific about being in jobs, relationships and communities that are large enough in spirit and diminishing to be in ones too small." Your vision is broad space; having one makes your work "salvific."

Holding a vision creates space for you to grow within that vision and it makes your work bigger than the institution in which you are employed. Without a vision, it's easy to spend all our time reacting to and attempting to solve an endless array of problems. We have no broader perspective in which to hold what happens to us. We look to our organizations for solutions and grumble that nothing ever changes. We inevitably become cynical, jaded, and burned out. With a clear vision, you're not trapped by the institutional mindset. Your organization will never feed your soul, but your vision will.

Your vision provides an inherently expansive view—a view that's nourishing and creative. It's a sanctuary that you can turn to for inspiration and support.

In the remainder of this book, we will be using the basics of learning that we've explored in this chapter: discernment, critical thinking, trusting ourselves, and being aware of what we are interested in. Learning requires an ongoing dialogue between your experience and your inner wisdom. In this dialogue, you pass information through an internal filter: *What does this material stimulate in me? Does it work for me when I learn? Do I think it will work for my clients or students? Why or why not? What is a next step I can take?* Allow your own learning to guide you. By letting the ideas simmer in the back of your mind for a while, you can observe the ways your mind wants to play with them. You may begin to notice natural associations. Whatever emerges will be your particular take on the matter.

Connecting with our inner voice is required as we traverse new spaces and places. Without a strong connection, we'd lose ourselves—overwhelmed by new information and experiences. When we have a way to connect with our own wisdom, we can hold a stance of openness. We are now ready and able to partner with the unknown.

REFLECTING
ON YOUR EXPERIENCE

Creating Space . . .

List three professional situations where you distrusted yourself...

1.

2.

3.

Do you see a pattern in these situations? For example, you may distrust yourself when you're verbally challenged by others or when your ideas go against the norm. Or perhaps there is a particular sort of environment that does not "fit" you or your vision. Spend some time writing about the pattern you see...

Describe a situation where you trusted yourself. How did it turn out?

List five things you can do to continue to strengthen your connection with your own voice...

1.

2.

3.

4.

5.

Renewing Inspiration . . .

Make a list of ten things you like to do that stimulate your learning and creativity. What situations, activities, and people move your heart? In her book, *The Artist's Way*, Julia Cameron calls this "filling the well."

> *One person wrote down:*
> *"browsing through a bookstore"*
> *"having conversations with Steve"*
> *"fly fishing"*

1.

2.

3.

4.

5.

6.

7.

8.

9.

10.

Write down how you will schedule at least three of these activities into the coming month.

Conversely, write down the places, people, or situations that seem to dampen your creativity and inspiration...

1.

2.

3.

4.

5.

Make an intention to make a change, so that less time is devoted to situations that do not "fill you up." Write your intention below.

Planting Seeds . . .

What moved you to become a teacher (or trainer, coach, mentor, workshop leader)?

What do you feel you stand for as a teacher?

What qualities or gifts make you unique?

What are four visions that you hold for your work?

1.

2.

3.

4.

Tending the field . . .

In this chapter we explored how the heart is important in teaching and learning. Where in your work are you half-hearted? Where are you closed-hearted? Are there any times when you are weak-hearted?

What changes might you make to put more of your full, open, and strong heart into your work?

The key to being a learner is to continue to notice what is occurring for you in your work situations. Also notice the sorts of issues you seem to be having with other people or organizations, and where you feel particularly emotional, because these issues will creep into your work. Here are some questions that you might want to ask yourself at night to help you keep "tending the field."

What inspired you today?

When did you find yourself having a reaction to something or someone?

What did you simply notice as being true for you?

What wisdom might you gain from today's events?

What is one thing you can do that incorporates this wisdom?

Digging Deeper . . .

Earlier in this chapter I introduced you to sentence completion exercises. As I mentioned before, it's helpful to repeat the sentence stem five or six times. Each time you repeat the question, you are digging a little deeper.

> *The thing that was neglected in my own education was...*

A trainer named Sherry responded:

> *The thing that was neglected in my education was... that I was a whole person.*

> *The thing that was neglected in my education was... that I wanted to have fun.*

> *The thing that was neglected in my education was... that there wasn't any point to what I was learning.*

*The thing that was neglected in my education was... that I
wanted to really be a part of something—like a family.*

*The thing that was neglected in my education was... that I
didn't think the way everybody else did.*

Simply let your pen write whatever it wants to finish the sentence.

A variation is to free-associate for a sentence or two with each phrase. So
for example, for the sentence above, "The thing that was neglected in my
education was...that I was a whole person," Sherry continued writing:

*I have thoughts and emotions and feelings and I need to be able
to express myself. When I was in school, I needed to be able to
develop my own voice and understand how I learn in this world.
These are things I can now incorporate into my work.*

Helpful Tip

When I'm in the middle of writing something that is not completely for-
mulated or doesn't seem to be flowing, I often write the phrase "And
what I really want to say is—" and then see what thoughts come off the
end of my pen. This phrase helps me when I feel stuck with my writing,
or when I'm not sure whether the writing is complete.

Create An Inspiration Board

Fashion designers often create "mood boards" before designing new collections. The mood board is a place for them to collect ideas for new designs; it includes colors, scraps of fabric, bits of jewelry, photos of exotic places that portray a mood for the design, and so on. It's a place to collect whatever inspires them, and keeping these items together in one place helps them to design cohesive collections that are true to their inner voice. But we don't have to be fashion designers to have inspiration boards—a physical reminder of things that spark our interest.

- Get a piece of cork board or a bulletin board that you can hang on the wall and push pins into.
- You might want to create a title for your board such as, "What Inspires Me?" or "What Do I Want?"
- Pin up anything that inspires you—ideas from books and articles, photographs, favorite quotes, drawings, images from magazines, small objects.

By using push pins rather than glue, you allow the board to shift and change over time.

CHAPTER THREE

Creating Imaginal Space

I find that, when a space is provided, something rather wonderful can happen.

— MAXINE GREENE

3

LEARNING AND THE IMAGINATION

MY QUEST OVER the past twenty years has to been to understand how adults learn in everyday life. After I finished
my Ph.D., I knew that I needed more than book learning. I
needed to know how *I* learned in the world, so I spent the next
decade throwing myself into new experiences in order to find
out. Probably because it is almost impossible to systematically
examine learning in everyday life, the standard academic literature typically investigates small, focused projects or the study
of a subject in school. When we're involved in something small,
contained, and pre-programmed, we may not need much space
for the imagination, but to learn anything of any magnitude
we need space—space that's full of potential and possibility.
You could think of it as breathing room.

While learning is typically associated with reasoning and thinking (in other words, the logic and linguistic processes of the left brain), scholars in many different fields have offered us a much different view. In their noteworthy book, *Metaphors We Live By*, George Lakoff and Mark Johnson emphasize the importance of the imagination in reasoning, describing the process as "imaginative rationality." Imagination is central to learning, because learning a concept can only take place to the degree that it is "reinvented" by the learner.

The philosopher Immanuel Kant called imagination the "third mental faculty." And some scholars have argued that Carl Jung considered imagination to be the fourth domain of knowledge. (The other three domains are thinking, feeling, and sensing.) Whether or not imagination is the fourth domain of knowledge, it makes sense to me that imagination is necessary for learning. Our imaginations provide us with inspiration, the necessary "fuel" to motivate inquiry. Our imaginations also bring *expansiveness*—new ideas, interesting connections, metaphors, questions to pursue and explore, as well as the fertile space to explore those connections. Certainly, the imagination must be a central component to learning.

Unfortunately, we Westerners have been quite dismissive of the imagination. "It's only your imagination," we'll tell someone. But other cultures are much more wise than we are. In *Dreaming the Council Ways*, Native American Ohky Simine Forest writes,

> Imagination is a powerful faculty that has been misunderstood by the Western mind. When you experience an extraordinary perception—let's say you heard a bird talking to you—if you tell this to a scientist, he would probably tell you,

"This is all in your imagination," as if it were nothing. But if you say this to a native medicine person, our answer would be, "Oh, good! So what did it tell you?"

The Sufi's believe that there are three "worlds": the world of our senses, the world of our thoughts, and something they call the "imaginal world." The imaginal world is the place where we receive visions, a place where Spirit can speak to us. It's a place in-between the physical world and the Spirit world, and from their perspective, it's a real place. It's not make-believe. In *Creative Imagination in the Sufism of Ibn Arabi,* Henri Corbin writes:

> For them the world is "objectively" and actually threefold: between the universe that can be apprehended by pure intellectual perception and the universe perceptible to the senses, there is an intermediate world, the world of Idea-Images, of archetypal figures, of subtle substances, of "'immaterial matter." This world is as real and objective, as consistent and subsistent as the intelligible and sensible worlds...The organ of this universe is the active Imagination.

Psychologist James Hillman said that all war is a failure of imagination, and this is true for any of our recurring problems. What moves us toward growth and positive solutions is having access to a more expansive set of possibilities—a larger frame of reference. Maxine Greene, a professor at Teacher's College, called imagination "the capacity to open spaces." And John Dewey said that imagination was our one capacity that helps us break through what he called "the inertia of habit" and see the world as if it could be otherwise. Imagination opens us up to consider new ideas. We step out from what we currently know so our world can get bigger, being limited or expanded by what we imagine to be possible.

In this book, I will use the terms imaginal, imagination, and imaginary interchangeably to refer to that special place of inspiration and unknown possibility. We could define the imaginal as a realm that is just beyond our ordinary intellectual capacities. It's the place that holds our growing potential. In the rest of this chapter we continue to explore elements of the imaginal—the making of imaginal worlds, image and metaphor, engagement with the heart, exploring unknown terrain, and the wisdom of process.

MAKING A WORLD

A FEW YEARS AGO I met with the president of a small university to inquire about teaching a graduate course. We sat down and spoke for a few minutes and then he asked me what I wanted to teach. "Metaphor," I blurted out. The topic was right there; there was no thinking involved. The word came out before I could stop it. The truth was, I didn't know anything about metaphor and I'm certainly not a linguist. I could have told him any number of subjects that I had prior experience teaching. But instead, something else spoke through me. Some wise inner voice knew that developing and teaching a class on metaphor would open up a new world. This is what I love about teaching. I get to *create a world* when I pick a topic that is deep, rich, and evocative and then follow the threads along with my students to see where they lead. (In this case, teaching a class on metaphor literally opened my students up to what the imaginal *is* in everyday life, and how it relates to learning.)

Sufi philosophers believe the imagination is real. It's not something to be dismissed. When we have a topic or something that holds real interest for us, that is something that's *real*. Your curiosity or wonder is not something that your mind has simply invented for no useful purpose. In his book *Balancing Heaven and Earth,* Robert Johnson calls our curiosities and fascinations "slender threads." He writes, "Slender threads were guiding me, and I would give myself over to their wisdom...It was not up to me to control the world around me; all I had to do was be attentive to its design and follow the slender threads." Our task is to trust these inspirations when we receive them. When we follow the slender threads, we open worlds.

Each of us has our own imaginal world, whether we are conscious of it or not. It's the place we turn to for inspiration, new ideas, and renewal. Our imaginations recharge our batteries, but they also hold our growing potential. They hold the vision of what we are "growing into." It's likely that the deeper purpose of teaching has to do with nurturing an individual's imaginal world. I once read a quote from Magda Cragg, who was speaking about her partner, the poet Lew Welch, when she said, "He made space around you, so you could grow." Let's all do that for one another.

IMAGE AND METAPHOR

OUR EVERYDAY LANGUAGE is full of metaphorical expressions. In fact, it's often difficult to speak more than a few sentences without using a metaphor. But metaphors are much more than fancy linguistic phrases. Metaphors allow us to understand and speak about things that are unknown, vague, or abstract. For example, we might say something like, "I'm in over my head" or "I'm just going with the flow" or "It's the point of no return." Most of our deepest life events (love, death, marriage, childbirth) are expressed metaphorically because metaphors are the only way we can understand our experience and communicate it to others. Consequently, metaphors are a central way we learn in life.

Metaphors offer us a mirror to see things that are hidden, or would otherwise be hard to see. Metaphors can expand or enlarge our view, but they also show us how our thinking has become narrowed, our vision limited. For example, a common metaphor in Western culture is "time is money." This metaphor arose in a capitalist system that assesses our daily hours in terms of wages, but other cultures view time very differently. Metaphors provide us with a way to investigate our assumptions and beliefs; they are an important tool for critical thinking.

Finally, some philosophers liken metaphor to the deep creative process that runs through everyday life. In 1949 Martin Foss wrote a little-known book titled *Symbol and Metaphor in Human Experience*, a book that has subsequently been called one of the ten most important philosophy books of the twentieth century. Foss writes: "...metaphor, compared to the clear, exact, and useful symbol, seemed unclear, complex, and useless—even as a superfluous luxury in the economy of the human mind. It was regarded as an ornamental addition. But what soon came to puzzle thinking men was how a supposed ornament could exert so dynamic a power in myth and artistic creation."

It's beyond the scope of this book to address the complexity of metaphor in everyday life, but what is true is this: Metaphors are a central way we learn in life and metaphors come from images. Metaphors typically arise from things that we can see or experience first-hand, things that are literal and concrete.

When we are born, our visual sight comes before the ability to speak. And of course, our early brains processed visual imagery long before we invented language. In *No More Secondhand Art*, Peter London writes that "Visual thinking and visual imagery is our *native language*" (emphasis in original). It's not surprising that our everyday language and thought processes are full of such imagery.

The late poet Stanley Kunitz said that poets have one or two favorite images that captivated them as children that they keep "working" over and over again in their writing. For example, as a child, E.B. White was fascinated by spider webs. He later went on to author the bestselling children's book, *Charlotte's Web*. Walt Whitman said it like this: "There was a child went forth every day. And the first object he looked upon, that object he became." Whitman was referring to the transformative power that images have on us when we are young.

A positive, life-sustaining metaphorical image gives us something to "grow into." In the vision quests that are common in Native American traditions, a successful vision supports a person for his or her entire life. The image that's received on a quest is a power upon which he or she can call for guidance and courage. One is always growing into it. Perhaps it's true that each of us, no matter our ancestral lineage, has a primary metaphorical image that guides us during our life.

A friend of mine, the product of two well-known physicists, grew up near the ocean in England. She, like her parents, is also a scientist of sorts. But her gift in her work offers to us the image of the ocean, and in particular, water. This deep metaphor of water and its fluidity is prevalent throughout her work and writings. For myself, my attachment to the earth and farming stretches far back in my ancestral lineage to ancient history in Norway. Farming, planting, and working the soil are not just images in my mind, they are actually something I live and breathe, despite having spent nearly all my adult life in the city. I'm fascinated by the concepts of "soil," "compost," "digging" and "planting," and I naturally refer back to these images when I need inner nourishment.

I often guide teachers through a visualization exercise that I first discovered in Parker Palmer's book, *The Courage to Teach*. I give them the sentence stem, "When I am teaching at my best, I am like a _____," and ask them to see what image pops up in their minds. The results are fascinating and instructive. The image usually speaks directly to the type of teaching they are doing. One man, who teaches classes in a federal prison, came up with the image of a tree. When he is teaching at his best, he is like a tree. I can't imagine a more wonderful image for prisoners, who not only need the strong roots that a tree provides, but also the natural beauty, strength, and symbol of growth. One woman who works with the aged at a nursing home came up with the image of a sparkler. When she is teaching at her best, she is like a sparkler. Several students who teach mathematics or computer software came up with the image of a magician.

Teaching at Your Best: A Visualization
(Adapted from *The Courage to Teach* by Parker Palmer)

Seat yourself in a comfortable position. Close your eyes and allow yourself to relax. Bring your attention to your breath, watching its natural rhythm of in and out. Exhale any tension with the exhaling breath. Relax your whole body, section by section, from the feet to the head.

Then ask yourself, "When I am teaching (presenting, counseling, parenting, facilitating, etc.) at my best, I am like a ___."

Do this quickly, and accept whatever image or words arise. Typically, what you get will be a metaphorical image that contains important information from your subconscious about your work.

> *My images have changed over the years. When I first began facilitating Stop Smoking seminars, I saw myself as a channel of love. That may sound goofy, but that's how it felt for me. When I just recently did this visualization, I saw myself as a cyclone—springing out new ideas, generating enthusiasm and excitement. The cyclone had the task of clearing out the old so there could be space for the new.*
>
> —a health educator

What is your image?

What are the qualities of this image in your visualization?

How do these qualities relate to your work?

Does this image suggest any changes for you?

It's interesting that thus far, nearly all the images people have received have represented life, creativity, and beauty in various forms. In his book *The Metaphoric Mind,* Bob Samples writes that metaphors from nature are much more powerful than metaphors from culture. (For example, childbirth is a powerful metaphor from the natural world; a clock is an example of a metaphor from culture). In my view, learning is closely linked to the creative process associated with the natural world. In some part of ourselves, we know how important creativity, beauty, and metaphors from the natural world are to invoke rich learning environments, but they are quickly forgotten when we focus on our slick methods and flawless presentations. Yet creativity and beauty are where the life resides.

In Chapter Six we will explore other uses of metaphorical imagery. For now, I simply wanted to show the power and value of image and metaphor. Metaphorical images offer us a world that's blooming with creative possibility, a world that inspires learning.

RICH CONNECTIONS

T.S. ELIOT, in commenting on Dante's *Inferno*, said, "hell...[is a place where]...nothing connects with nothing." For my own learning experiences, I look for interesting connections between things. When I was writing my graduate thesis, I looked for books that would inspire my creativity about the subject at hand. I made an effort not to spend too much time reading anything that bored me because I wanted to stay inspired. Non-scholarly pieces of writing, magazine articles, and children's stories secretly inspired me. Magazine articles on odd topics (topics that appeared to be far removed from anything to do with my own) often stirred up new thoughts. Stories, poetry, and artistic images evoked a deeper and more meaningful form of learning. I need richness and diversity to inspire my own connections, a richness and diversity that I often don't get when I stick to reading only the items on the prescribed list.

Think about the last time you picked up a research article that was written in a dry, factual manner, filled with charts and diagrams. You might have learned many things from reading this article, but the experience itself was probably fairly flat. On the other hand, the best books you have read may have brought in material from all over the place, making connections across disciplines, sparking your own capacity to make connections with the information. A well-organized research article might provide useful data and a good argument, but it's less likely to stimulate your creativity. Charts, while great at conveying statistics, are not likely to stimulate diverse connections unless more thought-provoking material is also brought in.

When I learn, I want inspiration and connection to something bigger—something that holds heart and meaning for me. I call this depth. Modern society tends to deny the importance of depth, maybe because it's hard to define. My definition would be something like this: We experience depth when we experience something in our hearts and body, as well as our minds, and when our feelings are invoked. Depth experiences can be momentary experiences of feeling profoundly connected to something or someone, and often to something that feels "Higher." A friend has told me about times when he was facilitating a group where he clearly felt that some "Higher Power" was "directing" him. I would call that a depth experience. Alone, I have had depth experiences while listening to a performance by the pianist George Winston and during my first experience of the San Juan Islands. I am sure you have your own collection of such experiences.

Things such as reference manuals or phone books that are purely sources of information are less likely to invoke depth experiences. For myself, I would rather sink into a historical novel or have a conversation with someone interesting at a cafe, than watch a training film. I would also prefer to attend a seminar that involves deep discussion and experiential projects, rather than a lecture format where I have to take an exam at the end. I would choose to read a personal memoir that interweaves scholarship with personal experience, rather than a textbook. These situations tend to be more expansive and provocative. Why? Because they have potential for depth and for connecting with my heart, as well as my head. Because my heart is invoked, I am more likely to be inspired and have new ideas flow through. I cherish this feeling of depth and I want it in my life.

Whether we formally call ourselves teachers, trainers, facilitators, coaches, or guides, we are responsible for the model of learning we are presenting. What kind of experience would you rather offer your clients or participants? What you are offering to them you are giving to yourself as well. We offer boring stuff and then wonder why we're burned out. Cold, hard facts are kind of draining after awhile.

There are many kinds of learning experiences in our everyday lives that are richly contextual. Simple examples include walking through an art museum or attending a poetry reading. While not every artistic experience necessarily opens up our learning, it's unfortunate that most learning environments have been so separated off from this realm. Douglas Sloan, a professor at Teachers' College, is one who has championed richer and more meaningful learning experiences. He writes in *Insight and Imagination*: "An education in which skills, narrow intellect, and information have no connection with insight, imagination, feeling, beauty, conscience, and wonder and that systematically evades all engagement with the great, central issues and problems of human life, is a wasteland."

You don't have to be an art or poetry expert to provide these connections for your clients, you only need to be open to them yourself. What you bring to your work will be uniquely you. Whatever connections are sparked within you will be appropriate for your participants. Seminar leaders may bring in popular films to teach architecture and design concepts; college instructors may have their students read novels for an urban planning class; or community leaders may show slides of gardens to teach principles of diversity at their organizations. You might connect your topic with biology, civic law, modern advertising, or 17th century Russian literature, whatever you have at your disposal.

The opposite of aesthetic, notes Caroline Casey in *Making the Gods Work for You*, is anesthetic. In other words, either we have a cultivated sense of beauty, or we are putting ourselves to sleep. Imagine that you are sitting in a meeting room, waiting to hear someone speak on some business or governmental topic. Imagine your delight when the presenter brings in something you weren't expecting, something aesthetic—a film clip, something from nature, a poem. Whether you appreciated what he or she was trying to do or not, a part of yourself has been newly invigorated. It was a breath of fresh air.

Obviously, no one is well versed in every field of endeavor, but people who love learning make connections across fields. When we learn in a narrow way we stick to the topic at hand, strictly keeping to a review of the pertinent sources. Inspired learning happens when we can make connections with other realms, because indeed, learning is about making connections. We learn about something by learning what it's like and what it's not like. Inquiring into diverse fields brings richness and depth to the process.

Any subject you teach has its corresponding examples in everyday life. While language is clearly part of everyday life, mathematics, computers, and other subjects are also part of our daily world. Our subjects surround us. A friend of mine who teaches elementary mathematics got the idea for a mathematics game from watching a dance performance. The dancers were initially lined up in two rows on each side of the stage, and then one by one they moved toward the center in a particular kind of rhythm. She realized she could have her students be like the dancers on the stage, but rather than dancing, each student would represent a number. They would move into the center of the room when they became part of an "equation."

A health educator often takes newspaper clippings with her when she conducts seminars at the local hospital. The newspaper articles provide fresh energy and they help her engage patients in current health issues. As another example, when I was an undergraduate I was required to take a Computer Engineering course. Our instructor got the idea for the class project while buying a soda. He assigned us the task of writing a computer program that would mimic the actions of the vending machine. The movie you just saw, last night's conversation, stories from the media, what you happened to notice while you were hiking with your dog this morning— examples of your subject are everywhere.

Allow time to see what comes up for you. When we ponder a particular question long enough, connections come in from a wide array of sources. Let your free associations meander a bit. See what connections the material inspires in you, and your clients will inspire new connections for you as well. Their questions and insights can trigger your own insights, which you in turn share with them. See how this works? An exciting learning environment is one where we keep inspiring one another.

Opening ourselves up to inspiration from broader realms of experience give us (and our clientele) the opportunity to make surprising new connections. I would love to see learning environments become places that provide the possibility for exploring another realm beyond the flat, surface level that we typically live in. Teaching and learning cut through the heart of life. We don't need to stay within the box.

ENGAGING THE HEART

N HIS BOOK *Acts of Meaning*, Jerome Bruner wrote that emphasis in our world has shifted from *meaning* to *information*, and
from the construction of meaning to the processing of information. This is particularly true in learning environments—
the focus is typically on information rather than meaning. It's
almost like there is an unspoken assumption that if the material is meaningful, it's not "intellectual." But as pointed out in
the last chapter, nothing could be further from the truth. In
fact, our loves, hearts, passions *drive* our intellects. The writer
Thomas Moore declared:

> We don't realize how much we have created a
> world where we've denied our heart. Computers
> and the Internet are heartless—they don't
> engage the heart. We need stories as well as
> data. We need artists and poets, and people
> who acknowledge humanity, people who are
> experts on the soul.

When we study various topics, we can look at the threads
that weave their way through our own lives. Teaching a subject
as if it's removed from our own experience creates an *anesthetic* environment. But when we see the threads of a subject
in our own lives and we follow those threads, we create an aesthetic learning environment. We create meaning.

Yet, you may argue, what about the technical fields, the
sciences? Surely, a computer seminar can't be meaningful. I
believe it can. The publisher Diana Vreeland once claimed that

without emotion, there is no beauty. Acknowledging whatever emotions are present for your clients is one important way to engage the heart. For example, if people are attending a seminar to learn how to use a computer program, they might be feeling some anxiety that they're not computer-savvy. Another example is the fear that people feel when they are training to enter new professions. They're embarking on something that's at least somewhat unknown to them. Addressing these emotions in a light-hearted way adds a rich and aesthetic element to your work. It gets everyone *engaged*.

Even if your seminar is full of seasoned professionals, there is emotion present in the room. How many of them are feeling burned out and stale? Burn-out is an emotion. It's something that can be talked about and explored. Addressing it would certainly rouse your audience. Sloan writes in *Insight and Imagination:*

> The neglect of those things that nourish the emotions begins quickly to have a dulling and deadening effect on the whole person. There is, for example, little to prevent a premature or total immersion in abstract thought severed from all artistic feeling from producing a dessicated and joyless experience of life. And once deadness sets in, a vicious circle arises from which it is difficult to escape.

We always have some sort of relationship with any topic we are studying. Often, personal feelings are involved, and uncovering these emotions, whether positive or negative, can greatly support our learning. We dive into mystery when we learn and we can learn to mine this mystery. For example, we can always journal about our experiences: *What happened to me today that speaks to this question? What was my reaction to X, Y, Z? How do I feel now? What is the question that is intriguing me right now? What gives me a feeling of excitement? Where do I feel some hope?*

Hillman argued that psychology's most mortal sin is its neglect of beauty. He writes in *The Soul's Code*, "By psychology's 'mortal' sin, I mean the sin of deadening, the dead feeling that comes over us when we read professional psychology, hear its language, the voice with which it drones, the bulk of its textbooks..." The same can be said for most learning environments, whether they be informal community rooms, corporate offices, or formal classrooms. The more we are able to satisfy the heart's need for beauty, the more inspiration we have available for learning.

EXPLORING UNKNOWN TERRAIN

VIEWING LEARNING AS a process of entering the unknown presents us with a different model. Most learning situations draw on a teacher- or leader-centered method, where the teacher, trainer, or group leader stands at the front of the room and is responsible for directing all activity. In this approach, the teacher/leader is the one who has all the information and wisdom. As a direct response to the teacher-centered model, some schools have experimented with student-centered learning approaches. In a student-centered model, students direct their own learning activities, the most radical example being "free schools" where students direct *all* their own learning. Teacher-centered and student-centered approaches represent opposite poles of the same issue. They are *polarities* and in Chapter Six we will discover a way to bridge these polarities. For now, let's explore a model that moves us beyond the polarities and respects that a greater wisdom may reside in the room, a wisdom that is larger than any single individual.

What I have found helpful are *subject-centered* and *group-centered* approaches to teaching. On most days, I want the subject and/or the group to lead the way. I want to be *surprised*—either by what the group brings up or by what the subject itself is bringing up for all of us. When I feel tired or burned out, I am even more likely to simplify my plan for the day and imagine how I can open up participants to something that's more expansive, welcoming the possibility that something meaningful will emerge. This may sound abstract, but it works. I view the class or workshop as sacred space. I give the participants more time for their own thoughts, I listen more deeply and openly, and I am more likely to follow their suggestions. I flow more.

Let's look at the group-centered model first. A simple description of group-centered teaching is that the instructor or seminar leader uses what comes up in the group for the topic of inquiry. Questions, comments, insights, and problems that are brought up in the group lend themselves toward new activities and new topics of conversation. Instead of the top-down model found in most educational situations, we can view the group as a collective that has a wisdom of its own. No matter what level of clientele you have, whether a bunch of pre-teens or grown adults, and no matter how large your audience is, this group has an inherent wisdom. There is a whole room full of people here with you—you're not all on your own. Use their knowledge and insights. They'll appreciate you for it.

A group-centered approach is nourishing. First, the group may do much of the work in coming up with the topics for discussion. It's hard to have all the energy and inspiration come from one person, i.e., you. It's also boring. Second, this approach is nourishing because the group can stimulate your thinking about the subject. After a great seminar, you get to spend the next few days mulling over what occurred. Inevitably, you will come into the next meeting with something fresh to discuss. Many tenured professors say that the reason they like to teach rather than spend all their time doing research is because student comments and questions stimulate their own thinking. This is an example of group-centered teaching. *Any* group, including a group of unruly adolescents, holds tremendous amounts of energy and this energy needs to be tapped. If you are open to what the group has to teach you, you will find an important source of continual renewal.

Similar to a group-centered approach is the subject-centered approach that Palmer discusses in *The Courage to Teach*. In this case, rather than *the group* doing the teaching, *the subject* is doing the teaching. In a teacher-centered approach, the teacher's agenda determine the course. In a group-centered approach, the group's ideas and preferences are given priority. But in a subject-centered approach, the subject is larger and more important than either the group or the teacher. Palmer writes: "Passion for the subject propels that subject, not the teacher, into the center of the learning circle—and when a great thing is in their midst, students have direct access to the energy of learning and of life."

In a subject-centered approach, we view student questions, audience comments, or whatever incidents occur in the group, as *the subject* teaching us. It has a kind of mystical or reverential feel, imbuing the room with a sense of the sacred. As Palmer discusses it, it's as if the subject is the "Divine Source" and we are here to be respectful and listen. We could imagine the Divine Source of Investments or the Divine Source of Solar Power or the Divine Source of Microsoft Word as being in the center of the room. What does this Divine Source want to teach during the course of your seminar? If Divine Source is too strong of a phrase for you, you might try "spirit" or "soul." What does the soul of your topic have to say about your current presentation materials?

In addition to noticing what the subject is stimulating in the group, you can also notice what is coming up for you. Notice what is going on within yourself when you are teaching or conversing with clients or colleagues. The occasional conflicts or disagreements can all provide valuable material and may be an important part of the subject's teaching. Perhaps you and a client hold different points of view regarding the material at hand, or perhaps he or she is causing some other difficulty. Whatever it is, you might be able to relate this conflict to the topic, providing a richer experience for both of you. Look for connections.

You can think of yourself as being a "container," a receptacle for whatever this subject wants to teach. You are taking the ideas and experiences that are coming to you and transforming them into interesting material for your students.

The subject-centered approach also immerses us in a sense of reverence and appreciation for the whole. In our technology-driven society, approaches to teaching often focus on learning sub-skills and then putting the sub-skills together. On the other hand, a gestalt is a pattern of elements that are presented as a whole, and the whole is more than the sum of its parts. Subject-centered teaching provides us with a gestalt approach to learning.

As an example, let me tell you about an African dance class I participated in at our local Y. There were two instructors— one taught us the first hour, the second was on for the second hour. For the first hour, the first instructor stood in front of us (about 50 students) with a microphone attached to her head. She had broken down some simple moves into sub-movements and she spoke through the microphone as she instructed us. She moved her hip to the left and we were to do the same. She moved her right foot out, and again, we followed. Move right hip, right knee, left hip, etc. I have never been a good student of dance, it's hard for me to follow, but she made it so simple that even I could keep up. I was bored.

After an hour, the second instructor showed up. This instructor brought three African drummers with her. The drummers set up their instruments at one end of the studio and soon we were immersed in wonderful and wild African drumming. This second instructor danced down the center of the room and told us to jump right in. We followed her, as best we could. I might not have looked anything like an African dancer, in fact, I am sure I didn't, but I was into the gestalt of it. I could *feel* it. I wasn't bored anymore.

I know. The first instructor was being a "teacher" and the second instructor was not. Even I had judgments about it. I thought, "She's not really *teaching* us anything." In hindsight, I was able to see how much she taught me. Without speaking, she immersed me in the experience of something she was passionate about and gave me a glimpse into the beauty and depth of African dance. When we teach, we can choose to be *instructors* or we can choose to be *guides*.

As guides, we may know the terrain but we can still be surprised. We provide a model for the learning process, set the boundaries on the inquiry, and show the way to proceed. The second African dance instructor provided that for me. Guides are not so much focused on imparting content as in taking us through a process. As guides, we get to immerse ourselves in the subject, along with our students or clients. We get to create worlds.

HONORING PROCESS

IN OUR EVERYDAY lives, learning involves moving out into unknown territory. We gather all the available information, make an informed decision, take action, and then evaluate the results. Learning is an adventure. We often have little idea how the other person or the world is going to respond to us. We don't know what kind of learning will occur, what new directions will open up for us, where we will be after this particular experience, or what is going to next strike our fancy. We might have some vague notions of where we are headed and how we might get there, but the rest is pure exploration.

If we allow time for silent reflection in a class or workshop, we don't know what will happen during that time. When we sit down for 30 minutes of creative writing, we don't know what images are going to come off the end of our pens. We have an *intention* to do some writing and be open to our creative process, we have a *place* to write our thoughts down, we have *time* set aside to do this process, and then we plunge— into unknown space.

But in most learning situations, we typically allow little time for stepping into this unknown space. Instead, we focus on filling: filling up the available time, filling up the participants' heads. As mentioned earlier, most of us are often overwhelmingly concerned about how we are going to present our material. It requires a different mindset to consider that we might be more responsible for *opening up the space* to allow unexpected learning to happen. Filling time is a much different approach than stepping back and allowing space to be present. The first way is draining; the second is expansive, even nourishing. And it doesn't matter whether your job is seminar leader or classroom teacher or workshop facilitator. In all cases, holding your work as a matter of creating space (and not filling time) is the nourishing approach.

I am constantly being reminded how important it is for me to respect and honor the wisdom of the process. The times I have been most unhappy with my teaching were the times that I did not allow enough of a pause, and instead I rushed on to the next thing without properly giving the topic at hand the time that it deserved. A generous pause gives both teacher and students time to see what *wants* to arise. Mystery is present in any learning situation. By honoring this mystery, you will be providing a richer experience for people—an experience where they have the opportunity to learn more about themselves and develop stronger learning skills.

Honoring the process will help you respect what is occurring in the moment. As a simple example, I recently led a seminar where each person was given ten minutes to pose a question to the group and lead a short discussion on the topic. My own view of this activity had been pretty routine—I would get (hopefully) some diverse perspectives, helping us come to a broader understanding of the material. But perhaps because each person had such short amount of time, the result of the activity led to a rich experience for all of us, as each person's question seemed to weave and build on the others.' Rather than 15 different perspectives that didn't fit together, the image that came to my mind was that we were piecing together a quilt. I had also planned to show a video that particular morning. But honoring the process we were in, I realized it was more important to continue to weave the quilt, rather than spend the remaining 45 minutes headed in a different direction.

Learning has an intelligence that is entirely its own. While content is obviously a central component, focusing solely on content forces us to make learning static. We divide knowledge into chunks and digest it. We don't pause to let the wisdom that is already there reveal itself. This static way of thinking about teaching has at least one sorry result: It inhibits the development of strong learners. It causes us to wait for "answers," not challenged to discover our own.

Renewing the Imaginal in Your Work

In adulthood, most of us start becoming bogged down by convention. We get used to following the unspoken rules in a given situation and forget why we're even doing things this way. Who came up with this particular set of rules in the first place? And why? We don't need to blindly follow along, doing things the way they've always been done. We can play and experiment, try things out and determine whether they work or not. In *A World Waiting to be Born*, M. Scott Peck writes that "perfect" states of unchanging Utopia have always failed, "maybe because they were insufferably dull."

What is dull to you? Here is my answer: Dull is predictable. Dull is being provided with the answers. Dull is not being allowed to discover, to explore the unknown, to get messy. We all want to feel life move through us. We want something that will shift us. Underneath their apprehensive exteriors, participants want new experiences, just as you do, even if at first they seem resistant to your funky ideas. We all feel some fear when we approach something that's unfamiliar. But just because we feel a little anxious or uncomfortable, doesn't mean we shouldn't participate. We're all here to learn, and the only way to learn is to take a risk and step outside of our protective shells.

So, drawing on the principles of the imaginal that we have explored in this chapter, here are some questions to get you started:

1) *How can you make learning a process of discovery?* Museums, literature, movies, field trips, and other imaginative venues can stimulate thinking and new ideas. In *An Intimate History of Humanity,* Theodore Zelden writes,

> ... curiosity has increased in modern times because of the stimulus given to it by the opening up of the imagination through literature and art, descriptive poetry, landscape painting and the cultivation of exotic plants. Every discovery opens up the imagination further, stimulating more discovery, it 'enlarges the sphere of ideas,' excites a taste for investigation...

2) *How can you help people uncover their own voice?* In the film *Dead Poets Society,* the schoolteacher character played by Robin Williams lambastes academic writings about poetry, and asks his students, "What do *you* think? Find your *own* voice." Writing, art projects, and guided visualizations are just a few ways that bring one's own inner wisdom to the surface. Creative work supports and develops the self, fostering the internal connections that are so important for learning.

3) *How can you provide beauty and "depth" experiences?* What is often missing in educational settings is a reverence for something deeper. No matter what topic we are teaching, we can look to story, metaphor, and other things from the aesthetic and spiritual/philosophical realms for inspiration. As Caroline Casey says, "When we make something beautiful, we

invite the invisible magic to live there." Beauty supports and enhances our work, and most of all, it's nourishing.

4) How can you take people's imaginations beyond the organization? How can you take clients on an internal trip beyond their current life situation and the parameters of the institution or organization you're working in? Boring instructional spaces deaden the human spirit. If you want to offer someone a true gift, you'll stimulate his or her imagination and sense of possibility in life.

5) How can you get people conversing and sharing with one another? According to psychologists, human beings have two primary relational needs: to express themselves and to relate to others. Toward that end, we can help foster connections between people, particularly among people who might not naturally gravitate toward one another. Standard ways for fostering connections include small group projects or other sorts of interactive activities. I also love doing various creative writing exercises that are related to the topic at hand. When the task is "creative" it releases the pressure people sometimes feel with a writing exercise. It's amazing how the act of sharing personal writing connects us all to one another. The community you help to build may have consequences that go far beyond your seminar or workshop.

6) How does the material you are teaching relate to your clients' lives? What are the most interesting and controversial elements of this material? People want real connection—not only with each other, but also with you, with the subject, with life. They want something meaningful. In whatever format in which you teach, a primary task is to connect people with the material in a way that holds meaning for them.

7) What can you do to shift or change the energy? Shifting the energy can mean something very simple. In her book *Wild Mind,* Natalie Goldberg shares a memory from her ninth grade English class. She writes that her teacher, Mr. Clemente, "read us Lawrence Ferlinghetti and Dylan Thomas as if poetry meant something. Then he switched off the lights. It was pouring outside." He told the students to put their heads down on their desks and listen to the rain. Goldberg continues, "I didn't know then that I wanted to be a writer, but I knew this was magic and I wanted more of it." Whether you coach, teach, facilitate, train, lead, or mentor, you have the opportunity to create magic for people.

8) *How can you use non-standard materials?* Bring in interesting items whenever possible. A friend who lectures on the topic of biological systems and community development often brings a piece of raw cotton to his seminars. He plunks it down and asks his audience, "What don't you know about this piece of cotton?" (i.e., we don't know where it was grown, who was involved in its processing, and so on.) Any simple object can shift the energy and encourage creative thinking. No matter what environment you teach in, non-standard materials are fun and thought-provoking.

9) *How can you get people up and moving?* It's always refreshing to be sitting in a business meeting or large auditorium and the speaker or facilitator tells everyone to get up and stretch. The more "formal" the situation is, the more people in the room, the more refreshing it is. I was once in an auditorium filled with 300 people, and one of the speakers led us through an entire standing meditation exercise. Just because there are several hundred people in front of you, doesn't mean they wouldn't like a moment to notice that they have bodies and to stretch them.

10) *Are you taking risks, experimenting, embracing the unknown?* Try stuff. It's OK if something doesn't work out the way you envisioned. Getting messy is much more likely to promote learning than polishing your prepared script. What you're trying to do is make a *connection*. If what you

try fails, you'll have a great opportunity to move the group to a higher level of creative thought. *Why didn't this work? What do you think would work better? What do you think would be the most fascinating and interesting way to study this material?* People don't learn via slick, polished performances. They learn when they have to think for themselves and connect with their own experience. So take some risks occasionally. They'll appreciate your effort.

11) *Are you being someone people can connect with?* Your participants or clients have to be able to see you. In other words, your heart has to be in your work. So, how are you when you teach, lead, or facilitate groups? Are you a real human being, sharing something that's important to you? Or, are you going through the motions? Great teaching is about being authentic. Czeslaw Milosz, upon winning the Nobel Prize for Literature, said, "In a room where people unanimously maintain a conspiracy of silence, one word of truth sounds like a pistol shot."

12) Finally and perhaps most importantly, *what is up for you?* Are you engaged with the material? Are you getting new insights and ideas? What connections are you making that you would like to share? The phrase "you teach what you most need to learn" is a truism. Bring whatever ideas you're currently "working" in to your seminars, lectures, and workshops. This will keep your heart in your work and people will respond to the energy that's present for you. Teach what you want to learn.

These are simply ideas to get you started. As in anything else, your own interests should spark your exploration. As Jung once said, "The creation of something new is not accomplished by the intellect but by the play instinct acting from inner necessity. The creative mind plays with the objects it loves." Working with other people in a teaching capacity gives you the opportunity to follow your own unique sense of adventure. Allow yourself to play with what you love.

UNCOVERING POSSIBILITY

L EARNING HAPPENS IN the respite between two worlds: the known world and the unknown world. A key aspect of being a learner is to be able to imagine possibilities in the unknown world. Simply creating room for new possibility will feed you. When we see no way out, when we feel the weight of the world on our shoulders, when we start feeling overly pressured and responsible for every little thing, we can quickly get drained. But when we give ourselves permission to open our imaginations, this feeling of spaciousness feeds us. This is not static world.

Just as a gardener scatters seeds, new possibilities are scattered throughout this book. They are the things that I find nourishing when I teach, present, or facilitate, and I hold them as possibilities for both students and myself. They include beauty, inspiration, and creativity; deeper connections with people; a sense of the sacred and connection to higher vision. They include the ability to know myself better and trust my inner wisdom; to grow in ways that make me feel stronger and more capable; to have my gifts and talents serve the world around me; and to take my learning and growth out into other areas of my life.

Whether your possibilities are similar to or different from mine, being open to new possibilities is a necessity if we are truly invested in this business of learning. Indeed, one could argue that learning is about being able to imagine possibility. Think about this in your own life. Aren't there times when you have been totally stuck? And didn't you finally begin to make some real progress the day you were able to see possibilities you hadn't seen before?

Whether your clientele are youth or adults, they hold potential like all growing things do. To be true to our craft, we need to stand in the belief that they can effect positive change in their lives and in the world. John Gardner, author of *On Leadership* and Secretary of Health, Education, and Welfare from 1965 to 1968, wrote:

> If one is leading, teaching, dealing with young people or engaged in any other activity that involves influencing, directing, guiding, helping or nurturing, the whole tone of the relationship is conditioned by one's faith in human possibilities. That is the generative element, the source of the current that gives life to the relationship.

If we have an expansive sense of possibility, we will be able to offer expansive possibility to others. If we don't have an expansive sense of possibility, our clients don't really need us. They can get information and training from books or the internet. If you work with other people in a teaching capacity, what you're providing is a belief in their potential, and this belief is what inspires learning. Your view of the unknown world matters.

Learning happens because we human beings can transcend ourselves. Seeing new possibilities, we're motivated to grow beyond what we currently know. In *The Everyday Work of Art,* Eric Booth writes, "The moment we see that the world we inhabit is not just a sequence of hard, dead surfaces with fixed absolutes, but that it also can be seen 'as if' it contains many non-logical truths, many mysteries, we head into a better future."

In this chapter we've explored the making of imaginal worlds, engaging meaning and heart, beauty, process, metaphor, rich connections, and the mystery of opening to something that's bigger than us. Every idea presented here can be incorporated in some way into formal and informal learning situations. As learners, we have the opportunity to partake in the adventure of the human experience. That is the kind of learning experience I want to have—one that celebrates my humanness. I hope you've started to uncover the possibilities that feed and enrich you. The things you give to your clients, you are also giving to yourself.

Perhaps you think your clients don't want to plow into unknown territory. Whatever your concerns are, your decision to explore new possibilities will do as much for yourself as your students. *You* need to be fed. *Your work needs to feed you.* What would most nourish *you*? One thing you have control over is what kind of environment you create. You can create a place where possibility blooms, or not.

REFLECTING
ON YOUR EXPERIENCE

Creating Space . . .

Look over the list of possibilities introduced in this chapter...

> Imagination
> Imaginal worlds
> Image and metaphor
> Making rich connections
> Engaging the heart
> Exploring unknown terrain
> Honoring process

What possibilities speak to you from the list above?

Pick one possibility that most appeals to you, and describe three ways you might incorporate it into your work.

1.

2.

3.

Renewing Inspiration . . .

In your life right now, what do you wish to learn?

What is important for your clients to learn?

How can you bring these two things closer together? In what ways can you incorporate more of your own self-learning into your work?

Planting Seeds . . .

How has the learning/teaching of this subject enriched your life?

How can you share this enrichment with your clients or students?

In this chapter we learned about following "slender threads." Are there any slender threads right now that are asking for your attention?

1.

2.

3.

Tending the field . . .

What is your view of learning?

Conversely, what was your parents' view of learning?

How are they similar or different?

My mother viewed learning as a way to "get ahead" and compete in the world. It was highly valued in our family, but more as a means of survival than anything else.

—Roger, computer trainer

My family belief system around learning was that science is good, and creativity is frivolous and bad. I grew up in a creative wasteland. Although both of my parents were smart and enjoyed intellectual pursuits, the reading that was done in our family was primarily utilitarian, like how-to books. Both my family life and my school life were nearly empty of poetry, art, and music. I learned to be practical and pragmatic.

—Beth, workshop facilitator

How might your view of learning influence the work that you do?

In what ways do you feel connected with your work? What is the nature of that connection?

In what ways do you feel disconnected from your work? What changes might you make to feel a stronger sense of connection?

Digging Deeper . . .

As discussed in Chapter Two, intuition is an important part of learning. I always use my intuition when I'm working on a paper or project, or when I'm developing class materials. I research and gather interesting ideas and then mull them over, letting the material tell me its deeper meanings. Our intuitions can do amazing work when we let them.

Perhaps the most challenging aspect of intuition is that we can't *make* it happen. When we try too hard, the guidance doesn't have any room to get in to our conscious minds— our thoughts and fears are crowding it out. We may have a specific question or challenge, but after opening ourselves to receive intuitive wisdom, we have to let go and see what comes.

I like to write my questions down on a sheet of paper and then store the paper in a special place. (I'll often write questions in the form of a letter: "Dear Wise One" or "Dear Creator.") Some people put their questions in a "God Box." I myself use a folded envelope made out of tin foil that I keep near my front door; I also have a special journal that's only devoted to asking questions. Whatever special place you have will be appropriate for you.

You can turn problems into questions and begin with "I Wonder..." For example,

- *I wonder how I can lead a great seminar where I leave happy and satisfied?*
- *I wonder what my students most need from this class?*
- *I wonder how I can get this project finished?*
- *I wonder how my work with this client can nurture and inspire me?*

After you've written your question, let it go. Don't keep struggling with it or thinking about it. You've turned it over to a more expansive and wise source. It's not your burden to carry anymore.

I've noticed that when my intuition is operating, it catches me off guard. I will be washing my dishes or watering the garden, and all of a sudden I have a flash of insight about something. I can tell that it's my intuition and not my mind "figuring it out," because the information came easily and effortlessly on its own accord. There is a feeling of wholeness and quiet strength about it.

Intuition is a bridge between the conscious mind and the unconscious—in other words, between what we know and what we don't know. When we relax our conscious minds (temporarily step out of what we know), we allow the unconscious wisdom to come through. More will be said throughout this book on this subject.

CHAPTER FOUR

Creating Space for Group Learning

What do I really need? And out went more and more things. Simpler and simpler. Stripped down, pared down, the house became alive.

— SUE BENDER, *PLAIN AND SIMPLE*

4

STURDY CONTAINERS

MUCH OF THIS BOOK is about the concept of creating space, because we need space for the expansion of our knowing to happen. In the last chapter we explored *interior* space—space for imagination, possibility, and new ideas. We discovered that we can't learn anything unless there's a place inside ourselves that can imagine it possible. This chapter is about *exterior* space, the space that is present between individuals in a room or auditorium, or between you and your coaching client or colleague. Exterior space is created with physical amenities, the timing of activities, ground rules, your agenda, how chairs are arranged, and so on. Without exterior space, the imaginal space that we developed in the last chapter does not have a way to flourish. Exterior space is created by having proper structure.

In *Necessary Wisdom,* Charles Johnston uses the term "container" for the structured spaces in his life:

> I spend a lot of time taking stock of and care of the containers I've created for my life: the physical places where I work and where I live, the commitments that define the relationships in my life, the kinds of things I choose to do. I find that, to a remarkable degree, if I just care well for the containers, what happens within them takes care of itself, growing and unfolding in ways that surprise and gratify... Things absolutely cannot grow unless they are in their own supportive environment. This means that you must grow a form that's nourishing of what you want to create.

Our need to care well for the container pertains to our work as well. The container is what shapes and forms what your work with another person, or group of people, will look like. The structure you create will largely determine how people will speak with one another, how they will address one another, how they will *be* with one another. Structure has great influence over how respectful they will be of each other's views and experiences. It will create safety, or not. It will create depth, or not. It will help facilitate learning, or not. Good structure creates a strong container for learning.

Structure is partly *physical,* created by four walls and the arrangement of chairs. It's partly *conceptual,* generated by the framework you build around your topic and the time you set aside for exercises and activities. Structure is partly *ideological,* in that it contains, in some way, the vision you have for your work. Structure also includes *how we speak and interact with one another*—having ground rules and other procedures that create space for democratic dialogue and the inevitable differences among people. And despite the desire many of us have to dismiss power as a factor in learning, structure also involves embodying your own *authority*.

Setting up a structure for the *process* of teaching and learning is more fundamental than the content you have to share. After all, if you want participants, clients, or students to know content, all you need to do is assign material for them to read and quiz them on it. Sometimes people are poor teachers because they know how to present information, but they don't know how to create a learning space. As you may know from your own experiences as a learner, good teaching requires both. We need some form of material, but we also need a strong container that supports our learning. In this chapter we explore how to create this container.

STRUCTURELESSNESS AND TYRANNY

WHEN I FIRST STARTED teaching and facilitating groups, I wanted to disband structure because I had suffered through so many years of feeling oppressed as a student. Oppressive structure is structure that has no purpose behind it. Bells ringing every 50 minutes; detailed agendas which one follows unequivocally; students sitting in straight rows not allowed to move from their seats. Oppressive structure is pointless structure.

Women are more likely than men to experiment with sharing leadership and having leaderless groups. Back in the

1970s, women were fed up with rigid, authoritarian systems. In feminist consciousness-raising groups, the common desire was to disband the tyranny of "power over" leadership. But an interesting thing happened: When authority was dismantled, another sort of tyranny developed. In these leaderless groups, the more dominant women—the most vocal, articulate, well-educated, and/or aggressive women—had more power than the women with more passive personalities and less articulate ways of speaking. These women discovered that it was not possible to eliminate the power dynamics within a group. Power was going to be present, regardless of whether it was instituted in formal ways by having clear leadership and guidelines, or whether it presented itself in informal ways. (See Mary Parker Follett's books *The Giving of Orders* or *Dynamic Administration*, or Robert Greenleaf's *Servant Leadership* for more in-depth explorations of leadership and power.)

A structureless arrangement was more likely to be tyrannical because the loose lines of authority allowed power to be exerted by individuals in hidden or manipulative ways. (See Jo Freeman's 1972 article "The Tyranny of Structurelessness" for an insightful look at leaderless groups.) Groups usually don't function well without some sort of leadership or rules of operation. If a group is set up as having no leader and no ground rules, then one (or more) individuals will take power and become the informal leaders.

Have you ever been in an unstructured group? Did you find it frustrating? A writing coach wrote the following:

> Last week I attended a poetry group. The leader didn't provide any guidance for how to comment on the poetry we'd written. (I'd been in other writing groups where the rule

was not to comment on the content, but only to comment on how it's written.) The poem I read was about a project I'm working on. The other poets responded immediately, giving me a lot of unwanted advice. It made me feel very uncomfortable because I hadn't wanted to open myself up for advice. I wanted to participate in the group to write poetry, not to get unwanted advice from strangers. So the next time we went around the group to read poems, I didn't read the poem I had written because it was something personal and I didn't want to get unwanted advice again. So I quickly wrote something that wasn't personal about my bike seat (of all things) and I read that instead.

These sorts of problems are easily addressed through the use of simple ground rules. An environment with soft or inadequate structure doesn't provide *more* individual freedom. A sturdy structure is what makes space available for people to share and learn from one another. Too little structure means that there are inadequate guidelines for how people can speak to one another.

From my own perspective, I believe that my need to experiment with sharing authority with my students stemmed from inner fear and insecurity about exerting my own authority. A friend of mine calls it "rank." I needed to step into my rank, because taking on the leadership role is what creates the learning space. It's what provides the ultimate structure for the class.

A few year ago, I taught a class of Ph.D. students who wanted to pursue careers in academic teaching. I decided that this was a perfect opportunity to experiment with all aspects of the seminar, including "lines of authority." After all, these were advanced graduate students at a school that was doing pioneering work in psychology. If I couldn't experiment here, I didn't believe I could experiment anywhere. (Can you tell that I like to push the edges?)

I presumed that the students had a level of maturity that could rise to the occasion of sharing the teaching. But after the first three meetings, there was division, acrimony, unhappy students, and my authority as a teacher had been severely challenged. It was definitely tyranny, as two aggressive students dominated the others. In order to realize my own goals for the seminar, I had to remain clearly in authority as "teacher." My desire to loosen the structure had created a situation where the structure was too weak to hold us. I went back to a formal teacher role.

Structure can be looked at as having both feminine and masculine qualities. In its feminine mode, it holds and nurtures us. It creates safety and ensures that people's individual voices are heard, supported, and strengthened. In its masculine mode, structure helps us manifest our intentions for the event, seminar, or workshop. Structure can do much of the work for us and it can create a space for beautiful connections to occur. Hopefully we will have a structure of high quality—not so rigid that it oppresses and not so weak that it creates tyranny.

SIMPLIFYING PLANS

A TRAINER attended a workshop on instructional techniques. In this five-day workshop, participants conducted daily mini-lessons that were videotaped. They were given strict rules for how they were to do the mini-lessons. Each ten-minute lesson was required to have five distinct parts. These parts were a bridge or "hook," a pre-test, an introduction, an active-learning lesson, and a post-test. Lesson plans consisted of writing down each step, including the actual sentences she would use to open and close the mini-lesson. Each piece of the lesson was divided into a specific chunk of time.

After she delivered her mini-lesson, the group evaluated my friend's performance and the evaluation typically centered on whether the lesson components were clear or not. My friend told me that she was so nervous her voice would shake. Lord help her if she should forget the post-test or the bridge. Needless to say, the experience did not facilitate much confidence in her ability to train. Lesson planning in this manner allows no room for flexibility and no room to allow the teaching to arise naturally. It creates the wrong impression that all we need is a lesson plan.

John Heider wrote a wonderful and wise book for group leaders, *The Tao of Leadership*. In Chapter 48 he recommends that we unclutter our minds:

> Beginners acquire new theories and techniques until their minds are cluttered with options. Advanced students forget their many options. They allow the theories and techniques that they have learned to recede into the background. Learn to unclutter your mind. Learn to simplify your work. As you rely less and less on knowing just what to do, your work will become more direct and more powerful. You will discover that the quality of your consciousness is more potent than any technique or theory or interpretation. Learn

> how fruitful the blocked group or individual
> suddenly becomes when you give up trying to
> do just the right thing.

Your clientele, topic, and professional environment will determine the extent to which you need to plan and the nature of that plan. If you teach snowboarding or teach people how to run a restaurant (like two of my past students), you might not have a written plan for what you're going to do that day. Whatever comes up during the course of the day is what you'll be teaching. You might have a general idea of what you'd like to focus on in a particular class and you do have specific things to teach, but since what you are teaching is a process, the process will take priority over any plan.

Most of us have some sort of a plan or agenda when we instruct or present material, but focusing too much on a pre-written script can disconnect us from what's actually going on with the group. Due to my anxiety, when I first began teaching in classrooms I'd spend hours detailing in advance each activity and what I would say. I've since discovered that it's more important for me to simply be present. The information is all in there somewhere and the words come when they're meant to.

As we've discussed, creating what you think is the perfect script will not make you a good teacher. Perfect-looking drills may look impressive to the outside observer, but they do little to facilitate learning. A degree of messiness is sorely needed to at least stimulate our interest. A teacher who was quoted in Johnston's book, *Necessary Wisdom*, said this:

> I've always said I wanted students who aren't
> afraid to ask questions and get a little messy
> trying to deal with them. I'm finally realizing

that if that is going to happen, I've got to be willing to get messy myself. I'm working at being better at not knowing, at diving into the questions with them, at letting myself feel confusion, curiosity, and wonder.

In the last chapter we explored the notion that we can view the subject as a "Divine Source" that has its own inherent wisdom. Simplifying the agenda (having more of a skeleton, rather than a detailed plan) is much more effective in bringing about a vibrant atmosphere for discussion, because by putting less emphasis on the pre-written plan, we give room for the subject to speak. We also get ourselves out of the way so that the wisdom in the group can come forth. We open ourselves and the group or audience up to a broader range of possibilities, possibilities that we couldn't have planned ahead of time. The vitality lies in the group itself, not in your pre-written plan. Besides, no matter how much pre-planning you do, the situation is probably going to give you something unexpected. You might as well simplify, and enjoy riding the wave.

CONCEPTUAL SPACE

ONE COMMON WAY that many of us are taught to have structure when we work with other people is to have written objectives. Written objectives provide guidance for what can be an unwieldy process and many of us are hired to teach or train specific blocks of information that can be easily measured and tested. Objectives may be necessary, but they are misused when they narrow our focus. When we learn, we need to be inspired (at least a little) and we'll never stay inspired with boring minutia. Our use of objectives can either stir up or dampen student enthusiasm. To motivate learning, we may need to open up the intellectual territory and encompass a broader perspective.

For example, suppose you teach English as a second language. Your students are recent immigrants trying to learn a new language and find employment in a foreign country. A set of objectives might be: *Lesson 1: to learn the verb 'to be'; Lesson 2: to learn reflexive pronouns;* and so on. The syllabus for this course would have 20 or so such step-by-step lessons. Such specific objectives offer students chunks of information that are easily measurable, but they don't create larger conceptual terrain for the course. They don't provide a rich learning environment for the students to step into. There is nothing in these written objectives to stimulate the students' imaginations or desire to learn. Narrow, easily measurable written objectives are boring. The more rigidly focused we are on achieving them, the more tediously boring our work becomes.

You have been hired to teach English as a second language, but you realize that your larger vision is to help your students develop self-esteem in both their language skills and in their ability to function in this new country. Indeed, these students are in your class to develop confidence in their abilities. Why not provide them with this larger intention for the course? They will certainly be motivated to work toward this goal. Your vision of self-confidence can be translated into a set of objectives, objectives that include the measurable results you also want to achieve. Some of these objectives might include encouraging students to speak up in class, assisting students in connecting their everyday life with the material, and so on.

What are other examples of broader objectives? Creativity, critical thinking, self-expression, community, leadership, and social change are but a few. Of course, you are teaching a particular subject, but you can use this material to move toward a more inspiring vision. There is a movie titled *Stand and Deliver* that's based on the true story of Jaime Escalante, a man who taught Algebra to inner-city high school kids at East Los Angeles' Garfield High. His vision was to develop self-esteem in his students and help them get out of the ghetto. The means for realizing this vision was Algebra. The study of Algebra was the means through which Jaime connected with his students and moved them toward higher self-esteem, his broader objective.

But in addition to sparking the interest of our clientele, other factors warrant broader objectives. First, narrow objectives are not an effective guidance system for how you will conduct the class, workshop, seminar, or training session. With narrow objectives, there is no larger view for how to proceed. You have no guidance for making choices about group assignments, seating arrangements, seminar procedures, and so forth. When you have a larger vision, each choice you make can be more conscious, moving you toward your goal. Broader visions provide better structure.

Second, when we narrow our focus to teaching easily measurable units of information, we have little opportunity for spontaneity, wonder, and surprise—the real jewels and joys of learning. Significant, transformative learning can't be adequately measured. How can you measure shifts in attitude, changes in perspective, openings in curiosity and wonder? When we focus on the lowest common denominator, we have little room to appreciate learning as a dynamic and creative process.

Third, it's a mistaken notion that breaking something complex down into sub-skills will then add up to a whole. We learn in a holistic, gestalt manner, not in a piece-meal way. There are a number of examples, including the learning of language itself. At some point, we simply have to plunge into the experience. The experience itself is what teaches.

Broader objectives create a large enough container so our clients, participants, or students can have their own inquiry with the material. We often have an end-oriented focus in educational settings. We provide both the objectives as well as the answers, and then we complain that people don't take responsibility for their own learning. Taking responsibility for our own learning means we pursue our own questions, develop our own inquiry, and have our own conversation with what interests us. You would do your clients a tremendous service if you could inspire and support this sort of personal learning quest. Learning is about discovery and the journey is motivated by one's own questions.

Many of us work in situations where there is no incentive to inspire further learning about a topic. Nevertheless, our deeper work is to *open up* the territory for learning, not clamp it down. Perhaps you could consciously vary the scope of your meetings with clients or students—sometimes using narrow objectives and other times having the goal of opening up the learning field by asking open-ended questions. Your objectives give you the opportunity to explore beauty, creativity, wonder, imagination, and all the wonderful things that comprise learning at its best.

So in that regard, a final important consideration is what your boundaries will be on the conceptual space. The material and scope of what needs to be covered creates a structure for your work. What is allowed into the intellectual terrain and what is not? Is the creative domain allowed? Is the affective domain allowed? As discussed in earlier sections, learning any subject brings up feelings and fears. Will you view students and clients as whole beings with a range of thoughts and feelings, or just thinkers?

A STIMULATING ENVIRONMENT

YOU PROBABLY DON'T need a research study to tell you that ugly, boring environments aren't good for our brains, but I'll give you some compelling evidence anyway.

Elizabeth Gould, a neuroscientist at Princeton University, started a new field called "neurogenesis" when she demonstrated that the human brain can build new neurons. It's innovative work, because for most of the previous century it was believed that we are born with all the neurons we will ever have. But Gould discovered something else that helps explain why prior researchers weren't able to see that our brains create new neurons. When Gould's primates were locked up in cages, their brains *stopped producing* new neurons. In other words, living in cages stopped the generative process for these primates. The way Gould described it was: "The neurons stopped investing in themselves." When the animals were given more complex environments that were similar to their natural habitats, the new cells that had begun to die, could be "rescued." Their brains started working properly again.

To translate this into human terms: Our brains are always giving birth. Natural, beautiful, and complex environments "feed" our brains, and support the production of new neurons. Ugly, unstimulating rooms, or environments where we feel trapped or constrained, stop the brain's generative process. In other words, we could hypothesize that ugly environments make us stupid, and beautiful (or at least, aesthetically interesting) environments make us smart.

So with the hope of creating more comfortable learning environments in this world, here are some things to consider:

- How quiet is the room that you work in? (Does the heating system make clanking noises? Are there voices that can be heard from the hallway or adjoining rooms?)
- Are there any other distractions?
- Is the room beautiful, aesthetically pleasing?
- How comfortable are the chairs?
- How calming does the place feel?
- Is there access to fresh air?
- How is the room lighted? Is there artificial lighting? Or natural sunlight?
- Is the room at a comfortable temperature?

We're more likely to learn when we feel comfortable and when the environment feels nourishing. Windows, sunlight, fresh air, and natural beauty do much to facilitate the desire and openness necessary for learning. But more importantly, our teaching is better as well. *We* need to be nourished. When we teach in aesthetically-rich environments, the place does much of the work for us.

ARRANGING CHAIRS

A FEW YEARS AGO a local church held an event called "Poetry and the Sacred." The invited speaker was the poet laureate of the United States. The event, conducted in the church sanctuary, was an hour and a half. The poet sat near the pulpit and spoke to the audience sitting in the pews. During his initial comments, he said he wanted this to be a conversation and that he didn't want to lecture to us. He read some poetry and then it was time for the conversation to begin. Inevitably, however, the intended conversation turned into a question-and-answer period. At the end of the evening, he pleaded that we work on the format for the series. He said, "It needs to be a conversation."

Why didn't a conversation work in this setting? One reason that was obvious to me was that we weren't sitting together in a way that allowed us to comfortably speak to one another. Despite the desire for such dialogue, we rarely seem to vary the format of public events. The main speaker nearly always faces an audience seated in rows. No rich conversation is going to occur in this kind of a setting, so why do we persist with this outdated model?

In some of my classes, students do practice teaching sessions. They have the entire room available to arrange in any way they wish. If they are given a room with a lecture podium and the traditional rows of chairs facing the front, the students rarely move the chairs. They do their teaching sessions as if what they have to *say* is all that's important. The arrangement of chairs is a simple element that has dramatic implications for how we speak to, and learn with, one another. The way we sit together matters.

The arrangement of chairs largely sets the conversational and power dynamics, determining how comfortable people will feel to speak up. The placement of chairs can easily cause one person to feel left out of the conversation, marginalizing him or her from the rest of the group. A participant in one of my classes, whom I will call Judy, described a seminar she participated in at a research institute.

The seminar was led by a well-known professor. Judy and two other people met with this professor three times per week to discuss their research findings. They sat together at a table— the professor at the head of the table and the two other participants on each side. With this seating arrangement, Judy, the third participant, was sitting on the far side of the table, next to another person but away from the professor. She felt left out of the conversation, because the seated positions of the professor and two other participants formed a triangle that excluded her. Years later, Judy still feels bitter about this.

Judy's experience demonstrates the importance of the seating arrangement in a learning situation. While some people might have the confidence to change the seating so that they are included in the discussion, many people accept the given arrangement without voicing their concerns, then feel angry about it later.

An important issue is to notice *where* you wish to create the learning space. The traditional arrangement with all chairs in rows facing the front obviously makes the presenter the focus of attention. With this seating plan, no matter what the presenter's intent, participants are necessarily passive. Of course, if you are making a speech to a large audience, there is little choice in the matter. On the other hand, if you are teaching an art or computer class, learning is probably focused on student projects, so space can be created at each individual seat.

I like to arrange chairs in a circle. This creates open space *in the center of the group.* The circle creates a center for our inquiry; we have a natural focal point, as if a shared intention were already present. The circle also creates the opportunity for meaningful dialogue. People can speak to one another freely and respond to each other's comments. It creates an awareness of equality—no one is disadvantaged and it eliminates the problem of sleepers. Every person has equal opportunity to express him or herself. The circle supports the larger goal of honoring individual voices and creating community. It shifts the power dynamic away from me being the sole authority, to the collective being the authority.

The Wisdom Circle

The origin of the circle format can be traced back to the days of King Arthur's Round Table, as well as to the council in Native American traditions. It has been used throughout history, from support groups, to feminist consciousness-raising groups, to group psychotherapy. The circle is used in a wide variety of settings—corporate, governmental, therapeutic, and educational.

In recent years, a number of books have popularized the Wisdom Circle as a method of conflict resolution, decision-making, and group process. The Wisdom Circle has a particular structure that creates the opportunity for deep, focused listening. Have you ever been deeply listened to in a setting that felt almost sacred? What happened? Did you find yourself saying things you didn't know you knew? Did you discover wisdom within yourself you didn't know was there? In Wisdom Circles, we not only learn from others, we also learn from ourselves.

What are the keys to a Wisdom Circle? The first is that only one person speaks at a time and there is no cross talk. Wisdom Circles, although they may have leaders, are structured and run in an egalitarian manner.

Second, an essential element is the "talking stick." The talking stick can be any kind of object that can be held in one's hands and passed on. The person who is holding the talking stick is the one who has the floor and the task of everyone else is to listen. Although one might chuckle at the thought of grown adults passing around a talking stick, the power of this instrument to evoke attention is remarkable. The talking stick creates room for the individual to speak and to receive from others a deep attention that is not typically present in a group. Often when someone is speaking, we listeners are spending our time thinking about what we are going to say or how we're going to respond. Or we're deciding that this person's comments are not worth paying attention to. Or we are mentally planning our evenings. Or we're thinking that we're bored and want to go home. The talking stick silences the unspoken noise and judgments, and creates a rich container for the individual voice to be heard. It's rare to be deeply listened to.

The talking stick is effective because it creates a *non-interactive, non-judgmental* domain for speaking. In many environments, listening to one another means *critical* listening. We pay attention only long enough to develop a counter-argument, our intent being to find the hole in the speaker's ideas. Critical listening is prevalent in everyday life—city council meetings, business offices, church meetings, board meetings, whatever. We humans are forever judging one another. We are nearly always open to evaluation, if not attack, when we speak in public settings. In the Wisdom Circle with a talking stick, you can speak with less worry that you will be critiqued, because the talking stick creates a feeling of sacredness. Your words are held as worthy of respect.

The talking stick creates a means for listening to oneself as well. Holding the talking stick, we may find ourselves speaking ideas that we weren't fully conscious of before. As Ivan Illich has written, it is "the silence in which we await the proper moment for the Word to be born in the world." Or in Ralph Waldo Emerson's words: "Let us be silent that we may hear the whispers of the gods."

A third key to the Wisdom Circle is to have a well-defined beginning, middle, and end, which further distinguishes it from random group chatter and everyday conversation. The clear delineation of time creates a container. There is a sacredness to this "bounded" time—an acknowledgement that we are now dropping down into a quiet, special place. This use of time is different from the mechanical time that is present in most business environments. Participants know that something out of the ordinary is occurring and they shift into a deeper place within themselves.

The Wisdom Circle has a few standard ground rules:

Withhold judgment. You may not agree with what someone has said, but he or she has the right to say it. Somebody else's view does not have to be right or wrong, it can simply be different.

Your job is to listen when another speaks. No crosstalk or speaking out of turn is allowed. We often want to respond to another's comments in order to show sympathy or show the group how wise we are. In a Wisdom Circle, our job is simply to listen.

When it's your turn to share, stay in your own story. Your story is where your wisdom lies. Speak in the first person, from your own experience, and from your heart, as much as you are able. We typically speak from our heads—from what we *think* we should say. Our minds can generalize and form opinions, but the heart is the place of true insight.

Be "empty." Allow yourself to not know ahead of time what you are going to say and just see what comes up. In a Wisdom Circle, there is no push to speak and there is no need to show how smart you are to prove yourself to others. Trust yourself and your own journey enough to allow whatever wants to emerge.

Respect the sacredness of this moment. This moment in time, with these people in this circle, is bigger than you are. There is something here for you to learn.

One common method for using a Wisdom Circle is at the beginning of a workshop as a method of "check-in" or introductions. When it's used in business or educational settings, it's often most effective as a way to close the meeting or seminar. If the seminar has been memorable or the participants have connected well with one another, the Wisdom Circle provides a way to honor everyone's experiences.

I will never forget the Wisdom Circle that I held on the last day of one of my seminars, as a way for participants to share more about their own individual teaching situations. It felt risky. None of them had ever done anything like this before, and there was definitely some giggling and awkwardness as they each spoke and then passed the talking stick on to the next person. But despite the awkwardness, or perhaps because of it, the talking stick quieted the group and they really *listened* when each person spoke. The room was pregnant.

One man, an instructor at a large state prison who had been very quiet up to that point, held the stick and started speaking of his work with prisoners. As he spoke, the emotions that he had been holding in—his compassion for his students and their situations, the darkness and tragedy of their lives, his efforts to help them—broke through to the surface and he cried. He had never been able to tap these feelings before, and here in this room where people were really listening, he had an opportunity to speak from his heart about his work. It was healing for all of us.

The structure you create may look very different from your colleagues'. Just as in architecture, where every building may be designed differently according to its purpose, structure in a group setting will look different depending upon what you wish to create. It will also vary according to the kind of group you have, the particular situation that's in front of you, and what your personality and teaching style are like. Develop a structure that is solid enough to hold the group's personalities, yet flexible enough to encourage creativity and depth of learning. As Johann Sebastian Bach once said, "Not the autocracy of a single stubborn melody on the one hand, nor the anarchy of unchecked noise on the other. No, a delicate balance between the two; an enlightened freedom." Like Bach, your own work is also a creative product. Let your vision inspire the appropriate structure.

REFLECTING
ON YOUR EXPERIENCE

Creating Space . . .

Let's explore your containers for learning in everyday life. In *Necessary Wisdom,* Johnston suggests the following:

> Take a few moments to look at the containers that play roles in your life–your commitments, where you live, where you work, the groups of people you spend time with. How effective is each of them in supporting the things most important to you in your life? Are there things you would like to change? New containers? Boundaries softened or made more solid? Larger containers, simpler or more selective ones?

Do you have structures in your life that no longer serve you, or structures that need to change? If so, describe below.

What steps can you take to create more appropriate structures?

1.

2.

3.

4.

Renewing Inspiration . . .

Can you draw any analogies between the sorts of issues and concerns you have for your everyday containers (your home, friendships, family) and the issues that are important to keep in mind when you teach, present, coach or mentor?

What practices might you institute that would help you create a stronger container for your work?

Planting Seeds . . .

What kinds of experiences do you want to have when you teach?

Pick an experience you would like to have, and muse about how it could happen...

List three ways you might provide a richer, more holistic perspective for your clients, colleagues or students...

1.

2.

3.

Tending the field . . .

What helps you prepare when you teach, facilitate, coach, or mentor?

Is there anything you find yourself doing that is no longer useful?

Are there any ways you can eliminate oppressive structure, replacing it instead with a more flexible structure?

On the other hand, are there ways that more structure, or a different sort of structure, would help you better achieve your vision?

Digging Deeper . . .

People often look at me in astonishment when I ask them to write a fairy tale, but I have found that this method of writing can be very helpful in going deeper into the heart of an issue when I feel stuck about something. Fairy tales tap our unconscious minds, often revealing, in whimsical and metaphorical language, hidden or unrecognized aspects of a situation. They often frame the issue in such a way that I no longer feel stuck, because I now see it in a new light.

Start by getting into a child-like place within yourself and write down the sentence stem, "Once upon a time in a land far, far away . . ." or something like that, something that conjures up the image of an old, old tale. Then, let your muse carry you in whatever inspired way it feels moved.

A financial consultant came up with this:

Once upon a time, in a tiny land that lived under a leaf...
The land was so tiny that there was nowhere to stand and so
people who were born there had to leave as soon as they could.
They had to go out into the big world and grow up. They had
to let the air and water feed and nourish them. They had to
trust that that would be enough.

I recently taught a Psychology of Metaphor seminar for advanced Ph.D. students. One of my first assignments was to have them write a fairy tale about the seminar itself. As you can see from the student's writing below, the fairy tale offers a way to playfully acknowledge the hopes, fears, and other unconscious issues that are a natural part of learning. There were twelve participants in this seminar, one of whom was pregnant, so he whimsically called the group "12.5."

> *Once upon a time there lived a crew of villagers who resided on the outskirts of town. 12.5 (Twelve point five) was their name and they were the fiercest warriors, best weavers, strongest woodcutters, finest artisans, and most effective farmers. One day, the King of the land became confused and began espousing the destructive nature of the 12.5. Many were in the King's command and they agreed with his words. The 12.5 were confused and shocked by the turn of events, as they were the source of the Land's power and majesty known throughout the world. To protect themselves from the impending attacks, the 12.5 agreed to go into the villages, disguised as Regulars. They took their divine skills and slowly taught the others the secrets of the 12.5. After many years, the 12.5 ceased to exist and they were called the Source.*
>
> – Steven

The stories come from a deep place of wisdom and they often provide clues for the direction that your inner self wants you to move. Whatever you get, don't judge or criticize your writing. It's all part of the process.

CHAPTER FIVE
Partnering With the Unknown

We can only serve that to which we are profoundly connected,
that which we are willing to touch.

— RACHEL NAOMI REMEN, *KITCHEN TABLE WISDOM*

5

LEARNING IS A CONVERSATION

IN THE 1920S, Lincoln Steffans was a history student at the University of California Berkeley. As a freshman, he became engrossed in history and read everything he could find on the subject. It soon became clear to him, however, that these scholars of history *did not agree*. He discovered that history was not a set of facts set in stone. Rather, history was an ongoing *conversation*, a conversation in which he himself, as an undergraduate, could *participate*. He wrote,

> What I had was a quickening sense that...every chapter of [history], from the beginning of the world to the end, is crying out to be rewritten. There was something for Youth to do...Maybe these professors, whom I greatly respected,

did not know it all. I read these books over again with a fresh eye, with a real interest, and I could see that, as in history, so in other branches of knowledge, everything was in the air. (Quote found in Danielle Lafrance's *Berkeley! A Literary Tribute*.)

We can only really know something by forming our own relationship with it. You can read a book on a particular topic and pick up various pieces of information, but the material will not come alive for you unless you develop a personal relationship with it—a relationship that inspires your own questions and responses. This is when learning becomes expansive. We don't know what this relationship is going to hold for us and we don't know how it's going to shift and change over time. In the process of developing this connection, we uncover our values and beliefs, which in turn shape our perceptions and subsequent learning. We also discover this particular topic's questions and areas of debate, footholds where we are most likely to want to participate in the conversation.

In *I and Thou*, Martin Buber wrote, "All real living is meeting" and that is true when we learn. Learning happens when we form a relationship with the thing we are seeking to understand. In Buber's words, we cannot "have" the ocean, we cannot have any *thing*—but we *can* engage in relationships in this world. We can enter into a closeness with other people and with things, and this relationship with "other" is what is transformative. There is a sacredness in this relationship, in this "space between" us and our subject.

In Chapter One we explored the idea that the base of your teaching is who you are, and in Chapter Two we examined learning as a self-reflective process that involves knowing what interests you, discernment, critical thinking, and trusting your-self. In Chapter Three we looked at the importance of imagina-tion, heart and meaning, aesthetic connections, process, and metaphor for learning. And in the last chapter we discovered how to create a sturdy structure in a dynamic learning envi-ronment. Now that we know that teaching requires a strong connection with our authentic selves, open imaginations, and a sturdy structure, we are ready to immerse ourselves in its intricacies. What is required when we teach in dynamic, con-tinually-changing environments—environments where we are working entirely with the mystery of human nature?

My approach is to be a learner, and just as Lincoln Steffans discovered in the example above, learning is a conversation. Learning happens when we move out of our individual bubbles to participate and interact with something outside of ourselves. Then we step back "in" to reflect on our experience. Breathing occurs in the same manner: in-breath, out-breath, in-breath, out-breath. As we move forward, taking steps out and in, we begin to develop our own relationship with the topic. In this book, we are exploring what it means to be teachers *and* learn-ers—in both cases, we ask questions, test them in action, and then go back in to reflect on what has occurred. In-breath, out-breath, in-breath.

The educator and philosopher John Dewey wrote that learning is a venture into the unknown which always involves risk. It requires courage, vulnerability, a degree of humility, and the willingness to be present to the unfolding. We may not know how to respond to some particular thing, but we are willing to learn.

STEPPING OUT OF THE ROLE

BEFORE I STARTED teaching, I was worried about the same thing every other new teacher worries about: What if someone asks me a question that I don't know the answer to? After all, I was supposed to be the expert, wasn't I? I asked a friend who was a university professor for advice. He told me that if he doesn't have a response, he derails it—he tells the person he'll be discussing that topic in a few weeks, or that it's beyond the purview of the course. But I didn't want to be elusive, nor did I want to shift the conversation away from legitimate questions.

When we operate in a teaching capacity, we are typically expected to be experts. But maintaining the role of expert is boring, and to the extent that there are heavy expectations on our performance, stressful. It's easy to feel nervous when we feel we have to be perfect. It's much more fun to be a learner, to be the doer. As learners, we are free to fumble and make mistakes. We are free to play, because our vision has not been narrowed by convention.

Most importantly, when we drop the expert persona, we're free to be ourselves. Hannah Arendt said that when people get together as *who they are* and not *what* they are, an "in between" space opens between them. I am more able to inspire learning when I'm simply being *myself* with people. I often share works in progress—current ideas, inspirations, and questions. I also hand out unfinished pieces of writing, writing that I am still mulling over, and ask for comments. My goal is to inspire learning and stimulate critical thought, not to be the expert.

When we're learners, we get to *have* the experience of learning; we get to have the adventure. In her wonderful book, *If You*

Want to Write, Brenda Ueland shares the story of a coach of a concert pianist who said of his student, "She always practices and never plays." Do you understand the distinction between practicing *at* something and actually entering into the experience? She writes, "When you are playing at it, you crescendo and diminish, following all the signs." But when our minds are totally focused on these mechanics, we're not having the experience of the music for ourselves. Instead, we're making sure that we do it right. We're playing intellectually, in our heads.

A wonderful example of *having* the creative experience is pianist Keith Jarrett's *Köln Concert*. When Jarrett performed (and recorded) that concert in Köln, Germany, it's clear from listening to the recording that he was totally into the experience. His performance has been hailed as a moving example of the creative genius at work. When you listen to the CD, you are taken on the journey with him. When we teach, we also need to allow ourselves to *have* the learning experience—an experience that includes the possibility of being surprised, excited, delighted, and every other emotion that goes along with learning. It's only when we enter *into* the experience that we have the capacity to be moved, and to move others.

MEETING AS EQUALS

IN MOST LEARNING situations, the instructor is at the top of the hierarchy; we don't often meet students as equals. What does it mean to meet as equals? We could partly view it as a matter of respect. Seeing someone as an equal means we see him or her as being worthy of our time. We are also more likely to be direct with him or her, not having the need to be shady or hide our real intentions. Meeting someone as an equal also means that we are willing to see the other as having something to contribute to us. Both parties are willing to listen and learn from what the other person has to say.

Meeting as equals may mean not letting fear get in the way of honest, direct communication. Many years ago I was an instructor in a program that was in the process of being reviewed by the state credentialing agency. As part of the evaluation process, the credentialing agency requested to speak to me and a few other instructors. For whatever reason (perhaps because my teaching style doesn't fall into the "traditional" category), I was nervous. I walked into the meeting feeling defensive, like *I*, not the program, was the one being judged. The credentialing experts immediately brought me to ease with their casual conversation and I loosened up. By the end of the meeting, we were "equals" with the same goal—having our program pass their review. The situation reminded me of something David Bohm once wrote: "We are not playing a game against each other but *with* each other."

An acquaintance told me about a weeklong workshop that he conducted at a nationally renowned retreat center. This acquaintance has written several books and he is an acclaimed poet and budding filmmaker. He had spent the entire week speaking about himself and his own work—he figured that was why they signed up for the workshop. On the last day, when participants were saying their goodbyes, he learned that several had also written books in the field. Somehow, he had missed an opportunity for the sharing of participants' gifts and for the rich conversations that might have come out of that sharing.

When we meet as equals, the social hierarchy is suspended—one person is not "lesser" than the other. You can see this quite often with medical practitioners. The last time you went to see a doctor, did you get treated as an equal adult or as a sick body? The roles we take on in everyday life may help us simplify our interactions, but they also cause us to shut off our minds and hearts and not see what others have to offer us. Keeping a hierarchical structure (parent-child, client-consultant, teacher-student, doctor-patient) creates distance and inhibits the simple fluidity that is necessary for learning. In *Making the Gods Work for You*, Casey writes, "People can be richer, poorer, wiser, less wise, older, younger, whatever, but the only effective form of communication is neither down nor up, but addressing each [other] straight across as an equal."

One of my most difficult students was an older man named Peter who attended one of my early classes. Peter monopolized the conversation. He spoke as the voice of authority, as if he was the only one who knew. When he wasn't speaking, he leaned back in his chair with his arms crossed in front of him and his eyes closed. (He made an effort to show that he wasn't listening.) Peter considered himself more experienced and wiser. Apparently, he was unwillingly sitting in this seminar because his boss required him to be there. I was unable to meet him as an equal, because he held himself apart from me and everyone else. Have you ever known anyone like that? The other person believes he knows everything and he must make sure that we know he knows. These people are unable to engage with us.

One extreme example of someone who was unable to engage on an equal level with other people was Adolf Hitler. James Hillman devoted a chapter of *The Soul's Code* to a discussion of Hitler's demonism. He writes, "The psychological trait that goes with the iced heart is rigidity, an incapacity to yield, to flow, to let go." Hillman quotes Robert Waite, a scholar of Hitler who said, "There was in his nature something firm, inflexible, immovable, obstinately rigid...Adolf could simply not change his mind or nature." The evilness in Hitler's nature stemmed from being unwilling to engage with or listen to other people. Hillman continues:

> ...Hitler had no use for exchange with others. There was nothing they could teach him. To show his omniscience, Hitler memorized masses of facts—all of which he used to overpower his questioners and embarrass his commanders. This information "proved" his transcendence and disguised his lack of thought and reflection and his inability to hold a conversation. The demonic does not engage; rather, it smothers with details and jargon any possibility of depth.

The comparison with Hitler might seem harsh, but it's an instructive example for deciding how we want to be with our students, clients, and colleagues. Conversation that inspires learning is a back-and-forth process. It's a creative give and take—each person is able to receive what the other has to say and build on it.

In *Waiting for God*, Simone Weil wrote that giving another our full attention is an act of love. She describes a way of attending to others where "the soul empties itself of all its own contents in order to receive into itself the being it is looking at, just as he is, in all his truth." And Lawrence Daloz writes in *Effective Teaching and Mentoring* that good teaching lies in a willingness to attend and care for what happens

to our clients, ourselves, and the "space between us." Good
teaching, in all its various forms, is a stance of receptivity,
attunement, and listening. Teaching and learning require
that we meet each other as equals.

BECOMING EMPTY

WE HAVE PROBABLY all heard the phrase, "the cup has to be
empty in order to hold something new." If we're all filled
up with what we already know, we don't have the empty
"beginner mind" that's necessary to see and embrace the new.
This section draws on material from M. Scott Peck's book, *The
Different Drum*, in which he describes several sorts of internal
blocks that can occur in group settings, blocks that hamper
our learning.

First, *expectations and preconceptions* fill our minds with pre-
set ideas about what a particular experience will be like. Peck
argues that as humans, we seldom go into any situation without preconceptions. Instead of allowing and receiving what the
class or workshop is offering us, we're busy trying to mold it
into our idea of what it should look like.

Our expectations and preconceptions create a narrow filter, causing us to dismiss and not see, hear, or experience what
doesn't fit the filter. Whether you are in the role of teacher or
learner, you'll enter a new situation with preconceived ideas of
what you think should occur. Groups may not conform to your
expectations or clients may tune you out simply because you're
not meeting some unspoken expectation. (It's always a great
idea to ask people at the outset what their expectations are. It

will get their preconceptions out in the open where they can be looked at and discussed.)

Pre-judgments arise when we create stories about other people, typecasting them into a pre-made role. We all do this. As learners, we decide who is smarter than we are and who is not. We decide who shares our point of view and who doesn't, and so on. We determine in advance whom we are going to listen to and whom we are not. Most of the time, we're not aware of what we're doing. We instantly decide to dislike someone based on the way he or she dresses or speaks and we're not even consciously aware of it. When we're in the teacher role, we may find ourselves making snap judgments about participants or clients—"This person looks nice," "That person looks like he doesn't want to be here," "She looks like she'll be difficult." These judgments get in the way of our teaching.

To teach well, we need to empty ourselves of prejudgments and let others show us who they are. Thomas Merton, the Catholic theologian, wrote in a letter to Dorothy Day that we must "look at the *person* and not at the *nature*...when we consider 'nature' we consider the general, the theoretical, and forget the concrete, the individual, the personal reality of the one confronting us." In *The Road Less Traveled*, Peck uses the term "bracketing" to refer to the process of setting aside one's own opinions and viewpoints in order to fully listen to the other. He writes,

> An essential part of true listening is the discipline of bracketing, the temporary giving up or setting aside of one's own prejudices, frames of reference and desires so as to experience as far as possible the speaker's world from the inside, stepping inside his or her

shoes. This unification of the speaker and listener is actually an extension and enlargement of ourselves, and new knowledge is always gained from this.

A third block to beginner's mind is when we use our *ideology and opinions* to try to convince others to see "the right way," which we believe is *our* way. Again, we all do this. In your particular field, practitioners and policymakers alike may hold strongly held opinions about what is right and what is wrong. In the education field, we often hear opinions such "lecture is bad," "small groups are good," or "class outlines and written objectives are good," "lack of structure is bad." Can you see your own ideology around your work? When we stay attached to what we "know," we can't see that there is a bigger mystery out there, waiting to be discovered.

Another block to beginner's mind is our human need to *heal, fix, or solve.* If someone has a problem we have been through, our natural tendency is to explain how we solved it for ourselves. But as Peck reminds us, our solution is not someone else's. Often, telling someone else our solution only makes that person feel worse. People want to be heard, not fixed. When we jump in with ready-made solutions, we're not listening. Instead, our mind is coming up with answers.

Learning requires a connection with one's own internal self, so pressing our own ideas onto someone else doesn't strengthen that person's connection with his own wisdom. Instead, try asking questions that allow the person to drop down more deeply into her own responses, i.e., *When did you begin to feel this way? What thoughts have you had about this? What have you tried so far? What do you need from this group right now?* And so on. To help someone else, we need to drop our own agenda.

Finally, Peck discusses the human need for *control*. Clearly, we want the participants in our groups or seminars to behave well and not be disruptive or antagonistic. We also probably want them to be kind to one another and ourselves, and to participate in what is going on. Most importantly, we want them to "get" what we are trying to teach. So what do we do in order to ensure these results? We control. We may try to control the group by avoiding conflictual situations or discussion items that aren't on our agenda. We may step around issues, maneuvering the group or the discussion in a different direction. I have found that my teaching is most effective when I step out of trying to control the group and take on an approach of "flow"—not "fighting against" the group's energy, but rather, yielding to what wants to emerge.

ALLOWING WHAT WANTS TO EMERGE

I N *SERVANT LEADERSHIP,* Robert Greenleaf wrote that the fundamental choice that defines leadership in all situations is the choice to serve life. Leadership experts stress the fact that good leaders *follow* more than *lead*. In *Synchronicity,* Joseph Jaworski writes that the "the deeper territory of leadership" involves collectively "listening" to what is wanting to emerge in the world, and then having the courage to do what is required. These statements remind me of an oft-repeated quote by Martin Buber:

> He must sacrifice his puny, unfree will that is
> controlled by things and instincts, to his grand

> will, which quits defined for destined being.
> Then, he intervenes no more, but at the same
> time he does not let things merely happen. He
> listens to what is emerging from himself, to
> the course of being in the world; not in order
> to be supported by it, but in order to bring it to
> reality as it desires.

When we work in a teaching capacity, we are also serving life. And life is naturally generative—new possibilities and realities are always arising. Good teaching is exemplified by how well one can see and support what *wants* to unfold in a group. Each group of participants will have its own character, its own personality, and its own issues. You can consider that the group has its own organic entity, its own soul. Your job is to serve this organic entity. What wants to emerge in this group? Where is the *life* here?

A group that has intentionally come together for some specific purpose is wonderfully fertile ground, full of potential and possibility. A typical response to this unknown terrain is fear—most of us want as little confusion as possible. But lack of confusion doesn't equal an interesting learning environment. In *The Leader as Martial Artist*, Arnold Mindell writes that a leader "is one who doesn't have all the answers, but is able to help draw the answers out of the group. It requires humility and courage because it's scary to admit you don't know." An exciting learning environment is one where we go with what occurs and see where it takes us. There is a charged feeling in the room, a feeling of both excitement and apprehension: *What is going to happen next?* People are *present*.

Chaos, ambiguity, and confusion are a natural part of any inquiry. We're not going to know ahead of time every event that will happen or every word that we will speak. Our words and actions will naturally arise from our engagement in the process. The good thing is that as learners, we always have the opportunity to step back, take a break, and reflect on and learn from the process. Although we may not know what to do next, we do have the capacity for *discernment*. We can ask: *Who or what is calling me in this moment? How am I being asked to respond?* We can throw out our old, outdated models of what we *should* do and ask ourselves: What *wants* to happen here?

Allowing what wants to emerge means loosening the need to be "in control" (in other words, in our roles, written agendas, and egos.) Our minds typically think they know how to fix things or that they need to be in charge to "figure it out." When we're genuinely present to whatever is happening in the situation in front of us, we create space for a greater wisdom to show us what to do next. The next right action arises naturally from our alignment with the present moment. When we simply show up and stay present, we have more wisdom available to us than we think we do.

Teaching is a complex business and there are no fixed ways of doing things. Our own intuitions serve us much better than advice from experts. The point is to reach participants using whatever works. When things don't go as planned it's an opportunity to throw away the model of what we think we're *supposed* to be doing and create something that *does* work. When we exert energy trying to push down or redirect whatever is spontaneously unfolding in a group, we can be quickly drained. A more useful approach is to let whatever is spontaneously unfolding, *energize* us.

In Chapter Three we explored the concept of subject-centered teaching. We can presume that there is an intelligence in this room that is wiser than we are, an intelligence that we can listen to, learn from, and surrender to. We are safe in this surrender because our ground rules, personal authority, and sturdy structure (developed in Chapter Four) are in place. My own journey has been about learning to trust this deeper wisdom, learning that my work is not all about me.

GIVING YOURSELF DEFINITION

ANGELES ARRIEN SAYS, "Not so rigid you lose your openness and humor, not so flexible you lose your definition." While too much control on your part can hinder and constrain what wants to emerge, you also don't want to lose your defined teaching space. You can't teach or lead effectively without proper boundaries. If you're spending most of your time and energy reacting to people's demands or expectations, you have lost your own space to teach. Putting the group at the center doesn't mean that your clients have power and you do not.

Our purpose is to offer those who attend our meetings, classes, events, or seminars what we have to offer them, regardless of whether they think they want it or not. They are here to be learners, which means that they are also entering the unknown. How could they possibly know ahead of time that they're not interested? What you have to offer your participants may be different than what many, or most, of them expect. That's OK. It's not possible to please everyone. You can't make everyone happy and you can't meet everyone's needs. Trying to please not only doesn't help the participants, it doesn't help you either. When we lose ourselves, we can't even reach the ones who are eager to hear what we have to say. Clearly, we need to give ourselves space to do what we need to do.

The only way for you to "allow what wants to emerge" is to stay true to your own voice, and only you can determine whether you are doing that. You might notice if you have shifted out of "listening" mode and into "reacting" mode, or whether you feel you have lost your own voice with your clients. Notice whether your actions seem to be driven solely by external demands and whether it feels as though your own connection to the subject has been lost. Only when you stay connected with your own voice, will you have something to offer others.

You can begin to create room for yourself by simply holding this as your intention. If necessary, you can visualize a space around yourself when you are in front of your participants, marking the boundaries of your own personal teaching space. With this intention, you are more likely to notice when you are moved "off center" by critical comments or demands. In *The Courage to Teach,* Parker Palmer says that each of us have an "inner teacher" that guides and directs our work. He writes, "The inner teacher acts as a guard at the gate of our selfhood, warding off what insults our integrity and welcoming whatever affirms it." When we work in a teaching capacity, we need this supportive, affirming foundation around ourselves.

Honor yourself. You don't have to respond to every person's opinion about your work. I often work with experienced teachers, so I get comments about my teaching. Most of them have developed a set of ideas about how teaching should be done. Some expect lots of information; others are active learning fanatics. One person was very adamant that a good teacher walks around the room and doesn't stand in one place. (He taught a group of students at computer workstations. Since this method worked for him, he thought everyone should do it that way.) People develop their own instructional methods based on their own personalities, subjects, institutional settings, and students. They may naturally feel these methods are universal and when I don't teach this way, their judgments come up. Giving yourself room to teach means giving yourself the freedom to do what feels right to you.

You can acknowledge and respect someone's opinion or input, but don't feel you have to shift what you're doing unless this feels like the "subject" is speaking to you. Again, this is a distinction that only you can make. In keeping with our focus on being learners, find a physical space away from your work where you can process what has occurred. A particular group may pose all kinds of new challenges—personal, interpersonal, and organizational. When you encounter difficulties, try journaling to disentangle what might be going on. Several suggestions in the next chapter will help you get started. You can also talk through difficult situations with colleagues who are more experienced.

Having an outside container in which to process what occurs helps us discover what our inner voice has to say. While we are in the midst of a class, seminar, presentation, or workshop, it's often hard to tap into our gut-level reactions and intuitions. Later, when we have time and space to reflect, we can carefully mull over the day's events.

No matter the professional setting—whether your role is instructing, presenting, leading, or facilitating—working with people in such a capacity can be intellectually, physically, and emotionally demanding. Burn-out is common among those who help others for a living. So what does this mean? It means that your first priority is to find out what nourishes you. What kind of environment feeds you? What kind of situation *renews* your energy and what kind of situation drains you? These are important questions.

Make sure that your structure is one that supports who you are. Some of us are well suited for large audiences, others of us work best in small, cozy settings. Some settings are formal, others are informal. The structure needs to support the sort of teaching you like to do and your unique talents and personality. What sort of structure enables you to shine?

Finally, part of giving yourself room to teach is having the opportunity to explore your own passions around a subject. Some people are happy to instruct or present material that's been developed by someone else. Others of us need to have more influence over the course content.

A trainer who worked for a large organization was required to lead weekly discussion meetings as part of her job. Although this situation might have been wonderful, in her case she had no control over the discussion materials. Having no influence over the material she was supposed to be discussing, combined with two difficult participants, made this a dreadful experience for her. If you find yourself in such a situation where you don't have control over the materials and it has become problematic, the best approach may be to try the "shape shifting" process described in Chapter Six until you can find a better match.

We create learning for others by standing in the truth of who we are and what we are here to offer. We are responsible for being authentic and having integrity with what we're doing, so that our students have someone and something they can connect with when they are ready. Having integrity means that we "walk our talk" and embody our professed values. This authenticity is what inspires people to learn from you.

SPEAKING THE TRUTH

CARL ROGERS ONCE wrote that the problem with most class-rooms is that people are fearful of getting involved (personally and experientially) in learning. Of course the same is true in learning situations outside of the classroom—from corporate meeting rooms to community events. The fear of getting personally or experientially involved causes us to be distant from others and the world around us, and afraid to voice our real thoughts. We keep our opinions to ourselves and interact with each other on a surface level. We don't share what we are noticing or speak what we are feeling. One or two people may dominate the conversation and no one says anything aloud, although we don't hesitate to complain to our friends afterwards. Or perhaps you were incensed by somebody's comments, but you weren't able to speak so you sat boiling in your seat for the remainder of the meeting. Were you listening to anything that was said? When issues fester under the surface, it's impossible to be fully attentive. In this section, we explore the possibility of making group process issues more of a conscious part of the educational experience.

What is group process? Most simply, group process is whatever human interactions unfold among participants in a group. Noticing group process would involve looking more deeply at what is really happening right now in this room: Who is speaking the most? Are some people actively participating and others dozing in the back row? Are men dominating the conversation? Are women dominating? Is one person monopolizing the conversation? Is this group allowing diverse opinions to be expressed? Does there seem to be a bias operating in the room? This is critical thinking on a group level—*noticing* what is occurring underneath and beyond the words that are being spoken.

Everything starts with the facilitator, so the skills of noticing also begin with you. Simply being aware of what is going on with you will help you when you experience difficult or tense situations. You can use "I" statements when you share with the group: "I feel there may be some tension in the room," and so on. If you speak from your own personal experience, no one can argue with or invalidate your feelings. For example, if you have a situation where one person is dominating the conversation, you can say something like, "I'm noticing some people are talking more than others. Do the people who have been more quiet want to say something?" You could also ask the group if they are comfortable with one person speaking more than others. Phrase your question in a friendly, curious way and not in a tone of voice that sounds critical. Remember: We're being learners, and learners are simply curious.

It can be empowering to verbalize what you're feeling. Howard Schechter says that by saying things that seemingly make him *more* vulnerable, he actually makes himself *less* vulnerable with a group. For example, I might prepare a talk or lecture that I know will challenge traditional belief systems. When I'm in this situation, I sometimes (unconsciously) find myself being defensive before I have even begun to speak! It's like I walk into the room with an armor of defensiveness already built up. If I follow the guidance in this section and speak what's true for me, it would be empowering to simply admit this to the group before I begin the talk: "I'm feeling a little defensive about some of the ideas I'm going to present today because..." Speaking like this brings everyone into the conversation and into the process. It wakes people up.

Or suppose you feel angry because you're not getting much participation from your students. I once gave a presentation where the audience members just sort of sat and stared at me (or so it felt). I couldn't get them to engage with me or with the subject I was presenting. The situation turned around for me when I took responsibility for my reaction. Because when I noticed and took responsibility for my frustration, I realized that *I* was the one who didn't have the energy or enthusiasm. They were just reflecting me—back to me.

If you're angry, bored, uninspired, or frustrated, people can sense it anyway. Noticing and giving voice to what you're feeling will clear the air, allow some humor to enter the situation, and give you an opportunity to shift in a different direction. You are never stuck in a difficult situation, because you're always able to speak how you feel about it. Speaking about the issue moves you into acceptance, and acceptance gives it the space to shift.

No matter what the situation, the beauty of saying *something* is that it then opens this issue up for discussion, and hopefully, resolution. It's likely that someone will say something to support what you have said and the conversation will continue to open. Most people are more compassionate than we give them credit for. Someone will likely respond to your comment by saying, "I feel the same way" or, "I noticed that too." Someone else will build on this person's comments and the ensuing conversation will move the situation toward more clarity. The point is that by speaking about what's true for you (or as close as you can come to it), you shift the energy. Once whatever it is, is out in the open, the issue has an opportunity to be healed and resolved, at least within yourself. It will not continue to fester under the surface.

If you speak what is true for you to the group, it can open up the conversation for everyone. This entire matter is not on your shoulders to resolve—others in the group will add their input to the mix. One of the most interesting discussions of group process can be found in Peck's book, *A World Waiting to be Born: Civility Rediscovered*. He writes,

> One of my techniques of group leadership was to repeatedly point out how the group was behaving as a whole and then gradually ask the participants to contemplate themselves the health of the group. It worked! The majority became increasingly adept at thinking in terms of the group as a whole.

You could start by asking simple questions: *What is getting in the way of our learning here? Was this activity interesting, boring, unnecessary? If you were the instructor or facilitator, what would you do now?* Your questions will get people comfortable with the experience of looking at their own individual process of learning, as well as the group's learning process. The situation naturally becomes more interesting and engaging for everyone.

Another idea is to give one person the job of monitoring the group discussion. At various points, the monitor can say what he or she noticed about the group interaction. *Did everyone get a chance to speak? Did two or three students dominate the conversation? Was there an underlying disagreement that didn't get resolved? Beyond the group interaction, what did this person notice about his or her own reactions? Did this person feel bored, inspired, annoyed? And if so, why?* Our personal reactions often provide clues about what is going on in a group.

In order for people to be willing to speak up, there needs to be a sense of safety present in the room. Unsafe terrain means that people are at risk of being labeled, judged, or deemed unworthy. Much of the safety for participants is created by your own emotional clarity, balance, integrity, tone, and demeanor. The way we say something is just as important as what we say. The truth-teller's task is to address the issue with sensitivity. We are less likely to create drama when we speak about something in a light-hearted manner— a manner in which our sense of humor is intact. Once again, we're simply being curious learners.

Finally, you might ask yourself or have your students ask themselves: *Why are you bringing this up?* and *Is this the right time to do so?* In order for learning to happen, insights that are under the surface need to be seen and acknowledged, but not necessarily right at this particular moment. Sometimes, taking note of it yourself is all that is necessary.

The skill of noticing what is occurring at a macro level is essential to learning. Further, by developing these skills we soon learn to better notice what is occurring in all of our everyday interactions. We can sense the quality of the communication in our personal relationships, or at the meeting at our church, or with the lunch speaker at the library, and so on. We soon learn to better differentiate and distinguish what we are feeling. We learn to be more awake in the moment.

HONORING DIVERSITY

A FRIEND OF MINE recently joined a group that's involved in various social change projects. One of the women in the group holds strong opinions about environmental issues and in the meetings she repeatedly says how nice it is for her to be with like-minded people. But her statements about like-mindedness made some members of the group, including my friend, feel unsafe. They wanted the freedom to think for themselves and come up with their own opinions. Having to hold themselves to someone else's particular set of views made them feel constrained and angry. In everyday life, we want to have the freedom to form our own ideas without getting others' ideas forced on us as the absolute truth. We want to think for ourselves.

I once attended a meeting and overhead a conversation between two seminar leaders. One of them said to the other, "No way. Not me. I don't allow people to disagree with me. If they don't like what I have to say, they can leave." Many of us don't allow much disagreement from our clients or participants. We have an expertise and a philosophy about that expertise and others aren't allowed to question it. But real teaching isn't about molding other people into images of ourselves. Our real work is about helping people learn, and learning is distinctive.

One spring, a student came to me and told me I had inspired him to give a lecture to his class of junior high students on principles of learning. It had gone very well and he wanted to thank me. He gave me a copy of the notes he used for the lecture. I read the notes and found many interesting ideas—none of which I had ever mentioned in class. This was not my material. I had simply inspired his thinking on the topic. I realized that this is what I had intended. I had wanted to create an atmosphere where students came to their own insights and conclusions—insights and conclusions that might be very different from mine. When we set up environments where people can tap into their own wisdom, then we are doing our work.

When we begin with the assumption that we are each different, we can find ways to come together and contribute to the whole without losing the diversity. I sometimes draw a picture on the board filled with an array of scattered dots. "This is your classroom," I tell new teachers, "try to get as many connections among the dots as you can." A participant who teaches at a state prison wrote in his final course paper:

> Most of my students are farther away from me—emotionally, psychologically, and intellectually—than they are with one another. I have found that trying to "connect the dots" has helped my class become a better learning community. Most of the students seem to work and learn more effectively from one another than on their own, so they work together in groups. Usually there is an individual or two from each group that is interested in the program and does have somewhat of a desire to learn. These individuals help connect the dots. Most of them have developed a negative attitude about receiving help from staff, whether it is worthwhile or beneficial to their lives or not. They tend to work more comfortably and listen more actively if a leader in the group leads the way.

No matter whether you are working with prisoners, business executives, or elementary school kids, some in the group will be farther away from you in a variety of ways. Participants are more likely able to learn from one another than from you. Create an environment where these connections can be made.

When we view our work as creating a forum for people to make their own connections, we honor diversity. How many of us grew up feeling marginalized because we were different? Wouldn't it be wonderful to start a trend toward allowing our clients, workshop participants, or group members to have their own distinct individual voices? This is how someone learns to think critically. As discussed in Chapter Two, critical thinking means we're digesting material and coming up with our *own* particular assessment of it; we're not regurgitating pre-defined ideas. In a best-case scenario, we're developing a unique set of ideas, a set of ideas that may be slightly different from the norm. Whoever your clientele or participants are, their interpretations of what you are teaching will probably look different from yours, but that's what happens with learning. Growth is about variety, and our role isn't to create copies of ourselves. Our job is to nurture the distinct voices that lie before us.

I will admit that I find it difficult when people in my workshops or classes disagree with me. And, I continue to find that the only effective approach is for me to take the stance of learner in this situation. *What message does this person have for me? What can I learn here?* Often, I find that I am holding a biased point of view and the person is offering me the opportunity to develop a broader perspective.

One method I have found useful for bridging ideological conflicts is the "Inner Bridgings" exercise in the next chapter, which has been very effective in helping me learn from people who have opposing viewpoints. You might try this exercise alone or with your clients when differences seem charged or insurmountable. But even if the other person's view is clearly wrong or misguided, if I take the approach of a learner I still gain wisdom from the situation. At minimum, if someone disagrees with me I can create enough space so that we both can voice our truths. It reminds me of what Rilke once wrote about learning together "side by side."

Research has shown that allowing space for diverse opinions actually accelerates learning for the entire group. Scientists have discovered that when people are presented with conflicting or incongruous information, dyssynchronous brain waves (indicating alertness) appeared. They concluded that conflict causes increased attention, and therefore, increased learning. Certainly, conflict helps us learn to think critically, because without a plethora of viewpoints, we have no way of learning how to distinguish between them.

We humans tend to fear what is different from ourselves. Since we are imagining new possibilities for teaching and learning in this book, let's imagine something that is more conducive to growth. How about coming to a place where another person's unusual ideas, instead of angering us or making us want to avoid him or her, *inspires* our own thinking on the matter? Upon hearing something that is radically different from our own belief system, we use this new idea to inspire our *own* ideas.

Healthy learning environments are places where people are allowed to think for themselves. In everyday life, we don't have to put up with people who disagree with us. We can just avoid people who think differently than we do. But while our communities and friendships are composed of those who are like-minded, you may have also heard the phrase, "Where all think alike, no one thinks much." Each of us have a unique perspective, formed by our background, past experience, interests, and personality. If you are responsible for creating a learning environment, of whatever form, you have an opportunity to create a space that recognizes, and even values, differences.

Our knowledge of something emerges through us, as we interact and have conversations with it. We do learn from others, but hopefully, we are taking what others say and passing it through our own filters. Having our own filter gives us a way to learn from someone who has radically different ideas from our own. The realm of "otherness" is where our true learning lies. In-breath, out-breath, in-breath.

REFLECTING
ON YOUR EXPERIENCE

Creating Space . . .

What do you need in order to teach (or facilitate, coach, mentor) well?

What kinds of things help you to listen to your inner voice?

What impedes you from listening to this voice?

Have you received any messages or clues lately from your inner voice that you feel you need to take seriously? If so, what is it, and what is it asking you to do?

Renewing Inspiration . . .

What are your personal edges, the places that feel risky and out of your comfort zone? Is it getting people to talk and share from the heart? Simplifying your detailed agenda? Lightening things up with some humor? One way to define edges is that they denote boundaries between things that you find uncomfortable or unacceptable (things that are outside of your comfort zone) and those things that are inside your comfort zone.

Write down three personal edges…

1.

2.

3.

Here are some examples of edges:

* *doing guided visualizations with clients*

* *having silence in the room*

* *partnering with someone to teach a seminar*

* *allowing some chaos*

* *being willing to change*

* *being in control*

* *being flexible*

You can use sentence completions to discover your edges. Continue to write until you feel done.

The thing that is most outside of my comfort zone is...

Are there ways in which you would like to grow beyond these edges? Write a commitment to yourself:

Planting Seeds . . .

Detach from this book for a moment and ask yourself what is really on your mind, preoccupying you, or taking up your energy. Spend some time describing this issue, exploring what is going on.

Is there a way for you to put elements of this issue into your work, so that you can learn more about it?

Business consultant Chris Argyris has developed a useful exercise that involves right and left hand columns of thought. The right hand column represents what has been spoken and the left hand column represents the unspoken—things that we think but don't say. Try using his method around your current work or teaching situation. On the right side, write down what you have spoken to your manager, director, students, colleagues, or yourself. On the left side, write down what you haven't said.

LEFT HAND (UNSPOKEN)   RIGHT HAND (SPOKEN)

Tending the Field . . .

Taking on the stance of a learner brings up the issue of how flexible you can be, and conversely, how much direction you need to provide. Let's take some time to explore your own experiences on the matter.

Try some automatic writing around these questions.

The ways I need to direct this group include...

My direction serves the group because...

The ways I need to be flexible with this group include...

My flexibility serves the group because...

Spend some time thinking about the times when you needed to improvise when you were teaching, mentoring, or facilitating. What happened? How did things ultimately work out? What lessons can you learn from these events?

The best way to improvise with this group is...

The way I can balance "messiness" and structure is...

How will you know when to become more flexible?

How will you know when you need to become more structured?

What signals are going to tell you to shift what you're doing?

Digging Deeper . . .

My favorite way to explore areas of concern in my professional work is to do a collage. This might bring to mind memories of elementary school art class, but I have found collage to be a deeply transformative process. It's the first thing I do when I'm struggling with something.

The process is easy. Get some old magazines (I get them for free from my public library), a glue stick, pair of scissors, and a large sheet of poster board. Go through the magazines and rip pictures that are evocative of the situation at hand. When I'm deeply in conflict, I like to use pictures of real battle scenes! Also clip words and phrases that speak to you. You might find the phrases naturally arranging themselves into a poem, but if they don't, that's fine too. Arrange the pictures and words on your poster board in a way that best represents the issue for you.

I find that simply the act of making the collage transforms the issue for me. There is something about making art that is deeply transformative. You often don't need to spend more time writing and processing, because the artwork naturally generates new perceptions. However, if you feel you need more process time, the next step is to do some journaling around the collage. Ask it what it wants to say to you and do some free-writing to get your response, or simply try doing automatic writing until you feel complete. When you feel you have received its message, find a place to hang your collage where you can see it. The act of viewing your "art work" on a regular basis is part of the process.

CHAPTER SIX
Cultivating Third Space

The teacher is a point of access to something beyond the teacher.

— PETER KINGSLEY

6

TEACHING IS A WAY OF GROWING

PSYCHOLOGIST CONDUCTED a study of people who like to play tennis. He said that initially, the participants in his study would say that the reason they liked to play tennis was to win. But then he asked them why, if to win was their real intention, they would choose to play with people who are better than they are? In fact, his participants nearly always chose to play tennis with people who were more skillful players, rather than people who were less skilled. His interviewees then admitted that the real reason they play tennis isn't to win, but because they like the challenge. In the end, we prefer to be challenged.

In *Getting Messy*, we have explored what it means to be learners. We have connected with our own voices, created inner space for new possibilities, created external space through appropriate structure, and we've immersed ourselves in the rich terrain that's available to us as teachers, facilitators, trainers, coaches, and mentors. As learners, our goal is genuine connection—with both clients and subject. The rewards and gifts of this approach greatly outweigh the costs, but there *is* a downside. The downside is that, by risking authentic connection, there is more opportunity for conflict.

Teaching and learning are personal; they're not impersonal. When we teach, we're naturally involved with something (some subject, person, organization) that we care about. And when we share our passion with others, we risk sharing our selfhood. We are vulnerable to being hurt, and our students are equally vulnerable. The tenderness of teaching and learning compels us to examine our hot buttons and inner conflicts, because they are often right on the surface.

We can spend our lives isolating ourselves from others or we can spend our lives learning and growing from authentic connection. Which would you prefer? In *Your Money or Your Life*, Joe Dominguez and Vicki Robin write of the Spanish word, *aprovechar*, which means to use something wisely. It's about getting the full value from life, enjoying all the good that each moment and each thing has to offer. We can hold that approach toward conflict as well. Challenges present us with an opportunity to grow and may offer important learning for the entire group. They're part of the journey and "grist for the mill." The people who set you off, the disputes that arise, the things that annoy and anger you, all hold important messages. *Why does this person bug me? Why do I seem to be at odds with this group? Why is this client annoying me? Am I trying to please my students? Have I abandoned my own voice here?* Issues come up all the time when we teach. They are constant. Each one provides us with an opportunity to learn.

I often hear writers remark that at some point before their books are published they go through a period of intense struggle with their topic, almost like an initiatory process. This is what happened for me. Two years ago I was severely tested by the most intensely difficult group of adults that I've ever encountered anywhere. Honestly, I didn't know how I was going to make it through. Although the twelve-week course was supremely stressful and took a tremendous amount of energy and attention, this initiatory experience (described in the "shape shifting" section of this chapter) taught me how to do something that I would never have learned in any other way. It taught me what "third space" is, and how to teach from that place.

It's all very well and good to think about taking risks and embracing the unknown when we teach, but what does this really mean? From my experience, it means that there is a "greater" place from which we can teach and learn, a place of higher wisdom that we can grow into. Otherwise, why bother to take risks and embrace the unknown? Why wouldn't we just go on doing the same old things? In fact, why bother to learn anything at all? Isn't the act of learning itself presuming that there *is* something greater we can move into? There is something beyond our current ways of knowing and thinking, something much more intelligent than we are. I call this place of greater knowing third space.

In the sections that follow, we meander through various sorts of conflictual situations that might arise between you and your clientele. In each of these situations, our approach is to be learners. We will presume that there *is* something for us to learn in this situation. And because we are taking this (humble) approach, a greater wisdom becomes available for us to draw upon. The inevitable challenges ultimately *strengthen* us, moving us and our work into greater depth, richness, and complexity.

AN IMAGINARY BOWL

URING THE THIRD class period of the first university course I ever taught, a man, perhaps ten years older than me, raised his hand. He said, aloud to the whole group, that if he had known what this class was going to be about, he would never have signed up for it. I felt like someone had slapped me across the face with a two-by-four. I went home, licked my wounds, and came up with a survey for the students to tell me what they felt was lacking in the class. The course turned out well— the other students did not share this man's opinion— but it was a good example of being publicly criticized in front of a group of adults. Ouch.

If you teach, train, present, or lead groups, you are opening yourself to the opportunity of being publicly criticized. If you are presenting something that challenges norms you will be criticized, but you'll also be subject to criticism if you have an odd personality, or a bland one; or if you have a curious accent; or if you walk funny; or if you grew up in Idaho; or whatever. When I began working with adults, I was unprepared for the fact that not every person was going to like me or what I was doing.

The best method that I have found for navigating critical comments is to imagine that a large bowl is in front of me and people's remarks are going directly into that bowl. It's a way for me to "hold a space" for whatever someone has to say to me. If I'm on a phone conversation or in a situation where I can do so, I may even put my hands out in front of me, so that I have a visual reminder that negative comments are going into this bowl. My imaginary bowl reminds me that I don't have to personally "take on" the other person's opinions or judgments (the bowl takes it instead). It provides me with a safe boundary and it gives me a way to acknowledge the comments, while also acknowledging that different people will have different opinions. The imaginary bowl gives me the personal space to say, "That's great advice. I'll take it under consideration." It also conveys the fact that I don't have to respond to all these remarks in this particular moment. I can consider people's advice or comments from a comfortable distance.

The imaginary bowl provides space for you to connect with your own voice without being unduly affected by negative commentary. This "imaginary" space is important for both teaching and learning—it allows us to connect with our own voice of authority.

PROJECTIONS

OUR TASK IN adulthood is to become whole human beings. Qualities that we don't like or can't admit about ourselves we often project onto others. Psychologists use the term "projections" to describe those qualities that we dislike in others and disown in ourselves. Other people might very well have these undesirable qualities, but when we find ourselves feeling angry or irritated, it's likely that we are projecting our own stuff onto them. Our task as adults is to integrate these disowned parts.

Projections are part of our everyday lives. The question we probably need to ask ourselves is not, "Am I projecting?" but, "Where am I projecting now?" Our task is to identify and own our projections. Psychologists will tell you that projections are a primary cause of conflict between people; they hinder our ability to listen and learn from one another.

Projections can be positive or negative. Your heroes and role models provide a clue to your positive projections. My hero is Martin Luther King. He is an amazing figure to me—someone who held to his convictions in the direst of circumstances. Although Martin Luther King is an inspiration to many, to the extent that I idolize him and put him on a pedestal, I disown the presence of these positive qualities in myself.

Since you're in a situation of being the authority figure, people will project onto you their views of authority figures, good and bad. People with positive projections will give you an undue amount of flattery and adulation, putting you on a pedestal and not owning their own personal power. In other words, they will be projecting their own power onto you. The problem with positive projections is that there will come a time when you (the glorified person) will fall from grace. At some point, you will do something fallible. Remember that a dynamic learning community is one where we meet one another as equals.

More insidious are negative projections, which are present when we greatly dislike some quality we see in another person. Let's say you experience a woman as being pushy and self-centered, and it makes you angry. She might very well *be* pushy and self-centered, but if you were not projecting onto her your own issues about being pushy and self-centered, you would notice her behavior and not feel much of anything about it. You would simply tell her to quit the behavior without feeling an emotional charge. The charge you get from it indicates that you are projecting.

When you don't own this quality within yourself, you get upset and react inappropriately. In this particular case, you are either disowning your own pushiness and self-centeredness, or alternatively, perhaps you need to be *more* pushy and self-centered in your life—you have not been as straightforward and assertive as you need to be. The anger or upset you feel gives you an opportunity to see how you need to grow and what you need to own within yourself. This person is giving you a gift.

It's helpful to be cognizant of your own projections with your clients, participants, or students and to recognize when they project onto you. You can't escape other people's projections. Perhaps you remind them of their father or mother, or the string of nasty bosses they have had. Or vice versa, you may see your mother or your boss in someone. The degree to which people are conscious of their anger or unexpressed issues will vary. In any case, to the extent that they are projecting on you, they will not clearly see you or what you have to teach. Has this ever happened to you? Have you ever had a participant in a seminar or workshop who was extremely difficult and it felt *personal*? Or perhaps it felt like someone didn't *like* you. When we work with other people in a teaching capacity, we're putting ourselves in a situation where we're exposed to their unexpressed issues and resentments—their projections.

In a later section, I will discuss severe resistance and what you can do about it. For now, let's review some general guidelines about being *authentic*. When we're open, we're less of a blank slate. In other words, when people see you as a regular human being like themselves, they'll feel more compassion toward you. If you're closed down and distant, it's more likely that other people will project their own unaddressed issues. So as much as makes sense in your particular situation, be a real person and view your clients as real people.

Being open and sharing what's true for you from your own experience is very different from sharing your personal troubles.

Clearly, it's not appropriate for you to burden people and waste valuable time on your personal life. The point is to be open about what is going on for you *right now in this moment*. If you feel uncomfortable or distant with some of the people in the room, you might find a way to share this in a light-hearted way. Each moment, be as real, present, and open as you can possibly be.

LEARNING IN DIFFERENT WAYS

THE MOST CONSISTENT conflicts that I experience often have less to do with the content of my ideas and more to do with the way I present material to other people. I am an intuitive thinker—I think in leaps and bounds. I am much more interested in the big picture than I am in details and structure. Some of the people I work with appreciate this approach and some do not. The way we take in and process information varies among people and those differences create conflict.

Drawing on Carl Jung's earlier work on the personality, Isabel Briggs Myers identified four dimensions of personality type: extroversion-introversion, sensing-intuition, thinking-feeling, and judging-perceiving. These dimensions became the Myers-Briggs Personality Type system. Of the four dimensions, the dimension of Sensing versus Intuition is the source of more difficulties and misunderstandings between people in every-day life than the other dimensions. The Sensor-Intuitive quality places the widest gulf between people. We tend to see those who are opposite us on this dimension as being "wrong."

Sensing-Intuition refers to the kind of information we naturally notice and absorb. Paul Tieger and Barbara Barron wrote an excellent book on the Myers-Briggs system, *Do What You Are*, that is a guide for selecting careers. Their descriptions of Sensors and Intuitives are helpful and this section contains a summary of their findings. Tieger and Barron describe Sensors as those individuals who take in information primarily through the five senses—they focus on what can be seen, heard, felt, and so on. "Sensors trust what can be measured or documented and focus on what is real and concrete."

On the other hand, Intuitives value the information they receive from their intuition over their five senses. Rather than focus on "what is," they focus on "what could be." Intuitives read between the lines and look for hidden meanings, possibilities, and relationships. They focus on implications and inferences. Unlike Sensors, Intuitives value imagination and inspiration over practicality. While everyone uses both sensing and intuition in everyday life, we each favor one method over the other.

Sensors are especially good at noticing and remembering facts, while Intuitives are good at reading a room and seeing the bigger picture. Sensors follow directions; Intuitives would prefer to dive in without instruction. Sensors naturally focus on realities; Intuitives naturally focus on possibilities.

Let me give you an example. I have a favorite bike path near my home in Marin County. The other day I was stopped by a cyclist who had lost his companions and needed to find his way back to where they'd started out. He told me that his group rode by an elementary school, and he went on to describe the school in detail—its color, the poles out in front, the slope of the street in front of the school. I've ridden my bicycle by this school perhaps 50 times, and I'd never noticed any of these things about it. It wasn't until I rode back with him that I knew for certain what school he was describing.

Sure enough, it was a yellow school with lots of poles and a sloped front drive. A Sensor pays attention to sights, sounds, tastes, and odors. To him, they are obvious and apparent. This is not the case with Intuitives.

Sensors	Intuitives
Trust what is certain and concrete	Trust inspiration and inference
Like new ideas only if they have practical applications	Like new ideas and concepts for their own sake
Value realism and common sense	Value imagination and innovation
Like to use and hone established skills	Like to learn new skills; get bored easily after mastering skills
Tend to be specific and literal; give detailed descriptions	Tend to be general and figurative; use metaphors and analogies
Present information in a step-by-step manner	Present information through leaps, in a round-about manner
Are oriented to the present	Are oriented toward the future

It's believed that Sensors comprise 75% of the population, while Intuitives comprise 25%. Thus, we can see why the institutions of our modern society have been built on the sensing model. Most organizations are not particularly focused on nourishing creativity or promoting the development of new ideas. Training classes, corporate seminars, tutoring sessions, governmental meetings, and so on, are based on the sensing model—they're well-organized with detailed agendas and clear procedural rules. Individuals who spend their time dreaming about possibilities have not fit in well.

Your working style will likely be aligned with your Myers-Briggs type, causing you to be more disconnected from people who are less like you. If you are a Sensor, you will naturally present information in a way in which fellow Sensors will understand. However, if you solidly stick by this approach, detailing your topic in a systematic way, you risk losing people who need to have their imaginations stimulated.

On the other hand, if you are an Intuitive, you will be more likely to present your ideas intuitively, using examples and metaphors, and seemingly going off on tangents because that's the way your mind works. You are the kind of person who likes off-the-subject questions, because you see it all connected to the whole. However, you may be frustrating the majority of people that you work with or teach. They will want to know what they are supposed to be doing, where they are headed, and wish you would quit wasting their time. These people are looking for a clear, straightforward structure.

As human beings, we naturally disapprove of behavior we don't understand and value people who have qualities like ourselves. So it's likely that if you teach, facilitate, mentor, or lead groups, you may be pushing your clientele toward your own way of processing information. It's important to notice how you are instructing and working with people. While we each favor either Sensing or Intuition, our task in adulthood is to develop a well-rounded personality. If your primary function is Sensing, it's desirable to work on your intuitive and imaginative capacities. If your primary function is Intuition, it's desirable to develop a greater capacity for presenting information in an organized and structured way. As you work on your own capacities in this area, you will be able to relate to a broader range of people.

Tieger and Barron describe how to go about developing your less-dominant Sensing or Intuitive capacities:

Developing Sensing

People who are developing their Sensing start to focus more on the present moment, taking things day by day. They become more interested in facts and details. They become more precise and accurate. They become better able to communicate their ideas to others in a clear and concise manner. They also become more realistic; becoming more concerned with how long projects take and with the realities of getting them done.

Developing Intuition

People who are developing their Intuition become more open to change and to seeing things in new ways. They become more interested in underlying meanings and spiritual concerns. They become more open to using their imaginations, and thinking about how people or things are related to each other. They start to see and focus on the big picture.

Knowing whether you favor Sensing or Intuition will greatly benefit your work. Generally, you are going to be much more likely to understand people who process information the way that you do, and you will have a more difficult time understanding people who don't. We tend to see those who have the opposite quality as strange, threatening, frightening, or simply peculiar and objectionable. We project our weaknesses onto others.

CONNECTING WITH INNER WISDOM

UNLESS WE ARE trained specialists in conflict resolution, the best that any of us can do when we experience conflict with other people is to work on it within ourselves. Often, when I draw on my own ability to learn and resolve the issue within myself, it becomes a non-issue for everyone else. As Martin Buber once wrote, "A person should realize that conflict situations between oneself and others are nothing but the effects of conflict situations in one's own soul." This section draws on the material in Chapter Two that explored discernment and connecting with our own inner wisdom. Our goal is to look at the challenging situation in front of us at a greater level of *depth.*

You might start by noticing your responses to the difficult situation. *What do you feel? What is going on with you?* You need to be able to sense and notice conflict, and then have the courage to deal with it, at least within yourself. Many of us have a fear of looking at issues when they come up in a group because they often tie into our own issues. We have to be willing to look at and deal with our own reactions and feelings. Freedom from struggle involves developing a larger repertoire of responses, rather than simply reacting.

It's often our unconscious reactions that generate conflict, rather than the particular issue at hand. In other words, *we* create the conflict by our response to the situation. Do you see how that is true? Otherwise, two people would simply disagree with one another amicably. Our attachment to our emotions and opinions creates the conflict. A marketing coach shared the following:

> I got angry when a corporate client wrote on an evaluation form that I was sloppy. She was referring to my (apparently) sloppy shuffling of papers. I went home and did some journaling. I saw that the reason I reacted to it so strongly was because it tapped into my own insecurities. A part of me felt like I *should* be neater and better organized. When I saw that my own issues were triggering me, I was able to not react to her comment. I was able to remove my anger from her and treat her just as casually as I did my other clients. And the wonderful result was, when I didn't react to her comment, nothing happened. I had no further problems with her. I learned that I didn't have to react and if I don't react, nothing happens.

If you're feeling embroiled with a particular person, you might ask yourself, "Whom does this person represent for me?" A young woman named Sarah shared this:

> I have to admit that in nearly every one of my workshops, a version of my mother is in the room. I don't have issues with my father, so I never feel discomfort with men in that

way, but I nearly always have a woman who acts and speaks to me in ways that bring me back to childhood when I was doing something wrong.

If you did the Teaching at Your Best exercise in Chapter Three, you have an image that can help you view disagreeable situations from a broader and more helpful perspective. This metaphorical image can provide wonderful wisdom to guide your actions. In *The Courage to Teach,* Palmer writes that his image of teaching at his best is a sheep dog. (When he is teaching at his best, he is like a sheepdog.) Parker used that image to give himself insight about a problem situation:

> Instead of letting that class unravel...a sheep dog would have barked and nipped at the wayward sheep early and often enough to keep them from becoming such a well-established distraction...A sheep dog would have practiced some form of "tough love" instead of playing the "nice guy" role until things got out of hand. I can translate these metaphorical meanings into all kinds of practical actions, from confronting students more directly about their behavior to using grades in extremis for behavioral modification. But the guidance I need, and the power I need to follow it, is in the psychic energy of the metaphor itself.

One of my students received the image of a concrete foundation, set sturdily into the earth. The image helped him realize that he just needed to create the foundation, and the rest of his work would take care of itself. Another person got the image of a channel. As a channel, her job was simply to hold the container (the channel) for the group and not be emotionally thrown off her center. Another client received the image of a bird, soaring freely through the sky. It helped her lighten up—she'd been getting too bogged down with details. Parker writes,

> This exercise, rooted in an image that arises from somewhere in my psyche, saves me from the quick technical fix I always want when I examine a bad moment in teaching. It returns me in imagination to the inner landscape of identity and integrity where my deeper guidance is to be found.

When you experience conflict, ask your subconscious for an image of "teaching at your best." The image will provide helpful clues for handling the situation, and a larger perspective that will help you grow into your best work.

In addition to working with the Teaching at Your Best image, you can also journal to uncover inner wisdom. In Chapter Two we did sentence completion exercises to help us get clearer about what might be going on in a particular situation. Writing about challenging situations from the third-person perspective helps us stay emotionally detached:

I see a situation where...

In this group is a wo/man who...

In the two sentence stems above you are writing about *yourself.* You need to know what's going on with you first, before you can address the situation in the group.

If you're having reactions to a specific person, you can explore those by writing:

If I were (so-and-so) I would be feeling...thinking...sensing...behaving...

These sentence stems are borrowed from Christina Baldwin, who has authored several books, including a book on journaling titled *Life's Companion* and one on circles titled *Calling the Circle.* In the latter book, she provides several other questions you can use to journal from:

- How have I been pulled off center?
- How am I contributing to any negative energies?
- What am I avoiding in this group or with this person?
- What am I afraid of? (What is the worst-case scenario?)
- Am I seeing this situation through a filter of past memory? Of judgment? Of fear?
- How can I do what's required of me in this situation and stay true to the spirit of this [seminar/workshop/class]?
- What truth do I need to tell? What's the most vulnerable truth I can tell, with no blame or judgment?

I find it most useful to change these questions into sentence stems, such as:

The thing I am avoiding in this situation is...

The way I'm being pulled off center is...

The thing I would like to do more of in this group is...

The biggest problem I have with this group is...

The thing that is true for me is...

The gray box that follows has a few other suggestions for resolving conflict. Also, check out the *Digging Deeper* exercises at the end of each chapter to help you get clarity on troubling situations.

Whether you teach, train, facilitate, coach, or mentor, you are being presented with people, along with their unique sets of issues, interests, reactions, passions, and so forth. Having a strong connection with our own inner authority is essential. The more clearly we are able to see the situation, the less likely we are to be thrown off balance. The more we are able to notice what's occurring, respond to our own reactions, and root out their source, the less likely this situation will set us off in the future. *What is this situation asking of me? How can I grow here?*

Some Ideas for Resolving Conflict

1) Try a period of silence...

> [Silence is] an implicit admission that all cannot be
> said, and that agreements are not perfectly possible,
> and that all the answers are not within our grasp.
> (Thomas Merton)

If a discussion is becoming polarized, you might press the "Pause" button. Retain a state of ambivalence, don't rush to make a decision. It's OK to leave it like that, leaving room for it to get resolved later. We are not pushing it down, but acknowledging it.

2) Try humor...

I always appreciate the lecturers, trainers, and public speakers who can turn an awkward situation into light-hearted humor. Whether it's forgetting someone's name, physically stumbling at the podium, losing your place in your notes, or any other sticky situation, you always have humor and light heartedness available to you. If you're feeling tense, look for the absurdity in the situation. Where you have lost your sense of humor is where your own attachments and issues lie. Better yet, go into the situation at the beginning with a healthy sense of humor. If it's not something you can do in a spirit of playful fun, it may not be worth doing at all.

3) Try making the problem bigger...

I once presented a seminar to faculty members in an unbearably hot room, but didn't say anything to the group about how uncomfortable it was. In this case, making the problem bigger would have involved speaking up and addressing the tension I was experiencing—both with the heat in the room, as well as my discomfort in not knowing what the faculty were expecting from me. I love this passage from Mary Elizabeth Braddon's novel, *Lady Audley's Secret:*

> There can be no reconciliation where there is no open warfare. There must be a battle, a brave boisterous battle, with pennants waving and cannons roaring, before there can be peaceful treaties and enthusiastic shaking of hands.

When problems are pushed under the rug or ignored they don't have an opportunity to get aired and resolved. This "elephant in the room" then diminishes people's attention and learning. Sometimes we might as well make the problem bigger.

4) Try stepping back and letting the group resolve the conflict...
If there is some sort of ongoing conflict occurring in your seminar or workshop, it often works best to step back and let the group resolve it. What's annoying you is probably annoying other people. For example, suppose someone routinely shows up late to your weekly meeting, disrupting the flow of events. If you allow time and space for group process and feedback, it's likely that someone will raise the issue for you. Every problem is not necessarily something that you need to bring up and resolve.

5) Try holding a council...
For deeper conflict, the Wisdom Circle (discussed in Chapter Four) may be a good choice. The council gives each person the opportunity to speak, while everyone else must listen. The talking stick provices a structure that respects each person's voice. Continue passing the talking stick around the circle or between the pertinent individuals until there is nothing more to be said. When done right, a Wisdom Circle will shift people out of entrenched positions into

more reflective perspectives. The issue may not be directly resolved on its own terms, and it may not need to be.

6) Try trusting the process...
When in doubt, we can try doing less and let the process take us where it needs to go. Gestalt psychologists often talk about "trusting the process," which means that the process has inherent wisdom and will show us the next step. In a subject-centered environment we are letting the subject teach us, so we can let the subject show us the way through conflict as well.
   a) Trust the process
   b) Stay with the process
   c) Get out of the way

7) Try connecting this conflict with the material you are presenting...
How does the conflict that's presently occurring relate to your topic? Are there significant points of disagreement in this field or subject that are displaying themselves in the room? If so, how do these conflicts get resolved in the larger world? Is there a way you can tie the present situation to broader issues, deepening the learning for the entire group?

8) Try being like a martial artist and deflect the punch...
In Aikido and other martial arts, you sidestep your attacker's force rather than resisting it. A martial artist never takes the punch full on, but rather, always deflects it. For example, suppose you are leading a public discussion and one person stands up and adamantly says you are wrong about something. Deflecting might look like this: "How do you think what I said does apply in this situation?" or "What do you think would apply?" These sorts of questions engage us in a non-defensive, objective conversation about the material. If we react defensively, it becomes a battle between us and the other person. "Our power lies

in remaining non-reactive," Schechter writes in *Jupiter's Rings,* "When we attack back, and defense is a form of attack, we initiate a war that no one can win."

9) For a polarized situation, try the "Inner Bridgings" exercise (described on the following pages.)

10) And when all else fails, try "shape shifting" (described later in this chapter.)

BRIDGING POLARITIES

AS HAS ALREADY been mentioned, both Jung and Einstein said that problems cannot be solved at their own level. What is required, they told us, is a movement to another "plane," another "field" where current problems diminish in importance and a new vision takes hold of the person. Einstein said, "The world we have made as a result of the level of thinking we have done thus far creates problems we cannot solve at the same level at which we created them." Jung said that the solution is to have a "higher" interest appear, in order to move our attention in a more expansive direction:

> All the greatest and most important problems of life are fundamentally insoluble. Some higher or wider interest appeared on the [person's] horizon, and through this broadening of his or her outlook the indissoluble problem lost its urgency. It was not solved logically in

its own terms but faded when confronted with a new and stronger life urge. (Quote in *The Collected Works of Carl Jung*.)

When you're in conflict with someone, you can view it as a situation where there are two opposing sides battling with one another. Sometimes, what we experience as criticism is simply someone who holds a different viewpoint than our own. Most of us see different viewpoints as a threat. We try to crush the critic or at least ignore him. Or perhaps we take the opposite approach and downplay our own viewpoint in order to appease and get along. A better method is to find the place inside your mind that bridges these polarities, which brings a feeling of "rising above" the situation. In *Necessary Wisdom*, Johnston calls the space that opens up when we bridge polarities "third space."

The basis for conflict could be any one of a number of polarities, such as work and play, masculine and feminine, thoughts and feelings, good and evil, success and failure, beautiful and ugly, freedom and control. As mentors, facilitators, teachers, and trainers, the potential polarities are numerous: Teacher-Student, Process-Content, Structure-Space, Individual-Group, Leader-Follower, Speaker-Listener, Mind-Body. Depending upon the degree to which we have already "bridged" this polarity within ourselves, we are likely to experience polarities as conflict. Johnston writes:

> To address questions of war and peace integrally, one must first have a solid start at finding peace with one's inner warrior and inner peacemaker. To address questions of gender in a creative way, one must find some degree of

creative marriage between the masculine and feminine within. And to address issues having to do with authority, the inner leader and follower, teacher and student...must have begun to learn to work together.

My bias when I began to teach was that I didn't see the importance of structure. I liked having an agenda that was sort of vague and undefined; I liked having a feeling of spaciousness and freedom in the room. Not surprisingly, my students wanted more structure and told me so. The "Inner Bridgings" exercise that I describe below showed me that I had a Structure-Space polarity that I needed to bridge. When I did the visualization, I saw Structure as a large, ugly, immovable, black metal object— kind of like a piece of industrial equipment. (This ugly image showed my dislike of Structure.)

Space, on the other hand, I saw as a wispy cloud that had a lot of energy and could move wherever it wanted to. But when I continued with the exercise, I came to see that the wispy cloud needed direction; otherwise, it was useless to me. The two images worked together— Structure gave direction and purpose to Space. Structure also had another important purpose—it could hold things. I saw that learning would not happen without a strong container. And Structure needed Space; it needed the lightness, energy, and freshness of the wispy energy. The two polarities—Structure and Space—needed and supported each other.

Often, comments that we experience as critical are useful feedback. By working with these seemingly critical comments, we can bridge these polarities within ourselves. For example, the belief that clients or students are being critical of you can be viewed as a Teacher-Student (or Teacher-Client) polarity.

What might bridge this polarity? In Chapter Three we explored the subject as the primary teacher; the subject is the third space that can bridge both sides.

You might want to do the Inner Bridgings exercise with your students or clients. When people disagree with you and there is conflict about it, you are probably each viewing the other as wrong. This exercise helps to bring the situation to a higher level of understanding and wisdom.

Inner Bridgings Exercise
(Adapted from Appendix I of *Necessary Wisdom* by Charles Johnston)

The exercise uses visualization. Since there is more than one step that you will need to read as you go along, it may be easier to have someone read the directions for you so you can just concentrate on the visualization. If there is no one around now, you can do it on your own. Talk aloud as you see the images in your mind's eye and jot down notes as you get information and insights.

1) Identify the Polarity
If you don't already have a polarity you want to work with, check in with yourself for a moment and see what issues in your life have some sort of emotional charge (anger, fear, confusion). It's not necessary to have words for the particular issue before you begin. It can just be some bodily or feeling sense that you have.

2) Setting the Stage
Find a comfortable place to sit, close your eyes, and get in touch with your breathing for a moment. Then imagine a stage, like for a play. Imagine that the two polarities you have chosen are two characters on

that stage and you are sitting in the audience. Let the images just come to you. They don't need to make any logical sense.

Notice everything you can about each of the two characters—what they wear, how old they are, how they move, and how they seem to relate or not relate to each other. Are they friends, strangers, antagonists? Let yourself be surprised by what you experience. The images may be remarkably clear and distinct or they may be cloudy or confusing. However they come, take them as they are.

Notice your feelings about each of the two characters. Reflect over the past year and get in touch with situations where one or both of them played a strong role. Notice if you find yourself siding with one or the other, making one good, the other bad, or making one important and the other not. Commonly, we identify with one half of a polar pair and disown and project the other half, seeing it as an attribute of others or of the world in general.

3) Engaging the Inner Dialogue
Start with the character you least identify with. In your mind, talk to it about the role you see it playing in your life and what you like and dislike about this role. Share with this character any thoughts you have about changes that might make things richer and more alive.

Then go over to where this character is sitting or standing, and sit or stand in its place. Let yourself become the character—sense its body posture, feel its feelings, notice what the world looks like through its eyes. Now, as this character, respond to what you said. Let the words that come out of the character's mouth surprise you.

Return to where you were seated in the audience and take a moment to become yourself. Respond to what the character said, acknowledging things that feel true and challenging the character where you disagree.

Then do a similar dialogue with the second character. Talk about the role you see it playing in your life and what you like and dislike about this role. Share with this character thoughts you have about changes that might make things richer and more alive.

Then again, take time to fully become the character and let it respond to you. Let yourself be surprised by what it has to say. Then once more return to your seat in the audience and respond back to what the character said.

Johnston writes, "You may wish to do a number of further exchanges as the feelings and content warrant. The dialogue opens creative, third space connections. And the act of going back and forth between the characters helps you understand in an immediate, visceral sense the difference between being in a third relationship space and being in a polarity. The hallmarks of the third space relationship are that you neither identify with nor disown either character. Another way to develop third space is to imagine how the two might work together. This does not necessarily mean being friends. Worthy adversaries can have a creative relationship. What would it look like if you were all relating in the most creatively potent way?"

After completing the above exercise, think about what you have learned. Reflect on what your "creative edge" is in relation to this particular polarity. What changes might you make?

SHAPE SHIFTING

RECENTLY I ATTENDED a fairly small (about 20 people) meeting in my community that had a speaker for the first portion of the meeting. What I noticed, while sitting in my seat, was that there were people in the room who didn't like the speaker. There were no verbal clues—the speaker wasn't being confrontational in her remarks and everyone was sitting there listening silently. I didn't know anyone in the audience, but I could still feel their animosity towards her. This is an example of resistance.

A friend of mine, an experienced and gifted instructor, is teaching a psychopharmacology seminar for graduate students in psychology. (The field of psychopharmacology investigates the use of drugs for the treatment of mental disorders.) The school she's teaching at and the students in her class are both "non-traditional," and for whatever reason, the students see my friend as "representing" the pharmacology industry. In fact, she's not associated with the pharmacology industry; she was simply asked to teach the course because she's one of the few people around who have the necessary specialized expertise. But the students can't see that. No matter what she says or how she responds, the students continue to view her as "one of the bad guys." This is also an example of resistance.

The people I know who teach, present, coach, or facilitate groups are in agreement on this point: By far the most uncomfortable moments are when certain people in the room are resistant to what we are saying or doing. Usually, I don't even know where the resistance is coming from, I can just *feel* it. Someone in the room is resisting me—someone is angry at what I'm saying or doing, or having some other negative reaction. When I am teaching or presenting in a room where there is no resistance, I am typically full of grace, ease, and confidence. I am joyful and happy because I love to teach and I feel grateful to be doing this work that I love. When I am working with an unsupportive group (even if it's only one person), I feel it intensely. My voice quavers. I am unduly anxious, I feel "off," and my words don't come out right. It's like my body is a fine-tuned instrument telling me whether a particular group is "safe" or not.

Like most of us who aren't trained psychologists, I don't have the skillful means of directly addressing whatever might be going on within the psyche of particular people. And even if I did have those skills, *I* am the target of this person's resistance. Being the target means that I am likely to be locked into this resistance as well, because to me it feels *personal*.

An acupuncturist described a situation when she was in acupuncture school. Her class of 25 students (nearly all women) loved and adored their male teacher. Then in the middle of the school year he quit suddenly due to some conflict with the administration. The students (of course) were plunged into heavy, dark emotional turmoil—shock, grief, fear, anger. Since it was the middle of the school year, he had to be replaced immediately. The teacher that was recruited was brought in from England. This woman, who had probably felt happy and excited to be coming to the States to teach acupuncture, didn't have a prayer. She walked into an angry group of students with no protection and I'm sure she had no idea what she was in for. Of course, the students instantly hated her; they were set up to hate her before she even stepped foot in that room. She was eaten alive. What did she do? She gave a normal human response—she hated them in return. The class was a nightmare. For the rest of the school year, venom and mean words were pummeled back and forth between teacher and students. Three years later, my friend is still reeling from it all.

My fire-walking situation that I mentioned at the beginning of this chapter was similar to my friend's, although in this case I was in the teacher role. I was brought in to co-teach a course at a school I was completely unfamiliar with. Little did I know, the students loved and adored the other teacher who already worked at the school. By the second class session, it was obvious to me that the students didn't want me there and they were going to make it difficult for me to continue. I considered ending my contract and letting the co-teacher finish out the course, but she didn't have the content expertise to finish the course on her own. I could have contacted the program director, but I knew she was swamped. And I could not morally bring in anyone else to replace me because they would be put in the same situation I was in. What could I do?

I believe that every situation is placed on my path so that I can be a learner, so I took the learner approach in this situation as well. I did the journaling exercises in this book to learn more about what was going on for me, but I knew that this situation was not only beyond anything my previous experiences had brought me, I also knew that the student reactions didn't have anything to do with me personally. After all, these students didn't know me. In other words, there was no "inner processing" I could do that would make this situation better, so I sought the help and advice of anyone who I thought could be helpful.

Although I got some interesting ideas, it wasn't until I approached advisor number five that I received advice that I thought could be of use. This advisor suggested that I "shape shift." She told me to move myself internally into a place of being "pure energy" and not my personality when I was in class with these students. She told me that by being my personality I would continue to stay locked into a polarity with them. Instead, she told me to "step out" of my personality and just be a sort of "pure energy form." She told me to spend time meditating before the class, getting in touch with the presence of this energy until I could really feel it. (Below I share the techniques that helped me get to that place inside myself.) "Make it an interesting experience for yourself that you will later use as a valuable tool," she said, referring to it as my personal "research project."

The idea was intriguing to me and I was curious to know if it would work. I also knew that this was my last hope. I had already tried confronting the students (two counselors told me to directly address the resistant students), appeasing them, shifting more responsibility to the co-teacher, and assigning a writing exercise to help students uncover the patterns they were bringing to the class. Nothing had worked. Psychically and energetically, this class of students was beating me up. (My friend Howard Schechter calls it "killing the teacher.") I also knew that if this method was successful, it would always be something that I could draw on whenever I encountered resistance in any form.

The next class session after my appointment, I drove to class visibly shaking. It took every ounce of courage I had to walk back in there. I stepped out of my personality and became "pure energy" and...it worked! Oddly, I even found myself joking with the students and enjoying the class. By the end of the quarter, the woman who had been nastiest to me was sweetly asking me for my advice.

The one caveat was that I truly could not be my personality. If I "slipped" and talked about something I cared about (was attached to), I was back in the painful polarized energy. This was difficult, because the class was on teaching and learning, two topics in which I feel passionately. But when

I stepped into my personality (in other words, slipped back into being someone who had a point of view), student resistance lunged at me in return.

The gift for me was that not only did I find an approach that worked, but I also developed a more neutral perspective toward this thing called resistance. Before this experience, resistance had seemed to be some awful intractable entity that I could do nothing about and that I would have to spend my time fighting in some way. By shifting out of the polarity, resistance became just a simple object that I could step around. And most importantly, it ceased to be something *personal,* something that was about *me.*

In the previous section, we gained insight from the wisdom of Albert Einstein, Carl Jung, and Charles Johnston, all of whom proposed that problems could not be solved at their own level. My exercise in becoming pure energy when confronted with severe resistance is an example of going into third space, a place where I could rise above the polarity, and when I did rise above it, the conflict was no longer an issue.

Even if the resistance is only coming from one or two people, if the polarity is strong enough the whole group senses it and picks a side. For example, the core projection in this case was good mother/bad mother. The students viewed my co-teacher as the "good mother" and me as the "bad mother." Even though this core projection was only coming from a couple of students (who I found out later had borderline personality disorders), the rest of the class (including myself) got pulled into the dynamic. From my perspective, it felt like the entire class was projecting this "bad mother" energy onto me. By moving into pure energy (third space), I offered the students in the class another alternative. They didn't have to pick one side or the other of the polarity. They could also rise above it into third space.

In learning how to become pure energy, one resource I turned to was Heider's book *The Tao of Leadership.* One way to step out of your ego personality is to imagine that you are a watery, fluid substance. If you have no fixed body mass (metaphorically speaking), there is no substance there for someone to resist. The wisdom in Heider's book is all about yielding to the resistant group in a fluid way that is like water:

> If gentleness fails, try yielding or stepping back altogether. When the leader yields, resistances relax...Few leaders realize how much how little will do.

> Never seek a fight. If it comes to you, yield, step back. It is far better to step back than to overstep yourself.

Another primary key lies in not being attached to what is going on (which can be difficult.) My experience with this taxing class was a clear demonstration of how attached I was to my own work and beliefs (despite how much I knew I was right!) After all, this was academia, where scientists pride themselves on being "objective." Even though I knew that true objectivity was a falsehood, I know now that I am a much better instructor when I detach from my own opinions. The more I let go of my attachment to any particular point of view or outcome, the less resistance I experience. Heider agrees that the leader should not take sides. He writes:

> Yield your position gracefully. Return to facilitating what is happening. It is not your business to be right or to win arguments. It is not

your business to find the flaws in the other person's position. It is not your business to feel belittled if the other person wins. It is your business to facilitate whatever is happening, win or lose.

You might ask yourself: *Are there places where I am pushing my own agenda? Are there places where I feel that I am right and I'm attached to my position? Is there a way I can step back, even though I think it's the wrong direction, so that I can flow with where the group wants to go?* The benefit of stepping back is that it will unlock you from the resistance. When you totally detach yourself, there is no longer anything for anyone to resist. And by stepping back from your "position," you are not stepping back from being "teacher." You are still teaching, but from a place of neutrality.

Clearly, being neutral contradicts my previous encouragement to be genuinely and authentically yourself, standing in your own "truths." I believe a primary solution lies in finding the right environment where who you are, and the sort of work you do best, are a match. When you find yourself working in an environment or with someone where who you are is not a fit (or you feel resistance to who you are or the material that you are presenting), you can "shape shift" into a place of neutrality and pure energy. When you do that you are also stepping out of your beliefs, likes, dislikes, and passions. In short, you are stepping out of viewing yourself as an "individual." (Incidentally, only individuals can harm one another in battle.)

The best two resources that I found to help me become "pure energy" with a group were the work of the English philosopher Douglas Harding and Eckhart Tolle's book, *Stillness*

Speaks. On Harding's website, www.headless.org, are a number of awareness exercises that I found helpful. When doing his exercises, I was able to shift into a place of realizing that who I am is not a body; who I am is an energy that is more expansive than my physical body.

In *Stillness Speaks,* Tolle writes:

> Artistic creation, sports, dance, teaching, counseling—mastery in any field of endeavor implies that the thinking mind is either no longer involved at all or at least is taking second place. A power and intelligence greater than you and yet one with you in essence takes over. There is no decision-making process anymore; spontaneous right action happens, and "you" are not doing it. Mastery of life is the opposite of control. You become aligned with the greater consciousness. *It* acts, speaks, does the works.
>
> When you fully accept that you don't know, you give up struggling to find answers with the limited thinking mind, and that is when a greater intelligence can operate through you... If words are called for, they will come out of the stillness within you. But they will be secondary.

Most of us have spent a lifetime acquiring specialized expertise, expertise that we are being paid to share and teach to others. And so it may be hard at first to grasp this notion: *The content of our thoughts, opinions, and expertise is secondary to the stillness within us.* That place of stillness is third space. You actually *can* teach a class, consult, or mentor from that place, and it's much better for everyone when you do.

On Harding's website is a quote from the philosopher Molinos: "Penetrate into the centre of nothingness. Creep as far as you can into the truth of your nothingness, and then nothing will disquiet you." I like ending this section with a quote on being "nothing" because this place of nothingness is where learning happens. When we already know everything and are completely invested in our beliefs, information, and opinions, we're no longer being learners with our clients or students. As I discovered with my most difficult class, I could teach a fine course from this place of being "headless" (as Douglas Harding calls it). A friend of mine told me recently, "If your work doesn't come when you're headless, then it's not your *real* work."

KEEP YOUR FORM

MUCH OF THIS BOOK has been about "keeping our form," yet the last two sections seem to be about "losing our form." To help explain this, let me give you an analogy I learned from Howard Schechter. Howard says that long distance runners reach a point before the finish line where every cell in their body wants to collapse. But the runners can't give in to the impulse to quit, they have to push through it. If they push through it, they eventually find a fresh pocket of energy that allows them to finish the race. As trainers, teachers, facilitators, mentors, coaches, and group leaders, we also need to keep our form. You might experience many moments when you want to collapse, or storm out of the room, or quit mid-semester. (I had my resignation letter to the Program Director all prepared and ready to go.) Instead of giving in to this impulse, stay with your form. You'll come out much wiser in the end.

Oddly enough, in the situation described above, in order for me to *keep* my form, I had to stay in a third space of being pure energy. If I stepped back into the polarity, I would have definitely lost my form. I would have crumbled. The third space of pure energy allowed me to maintain my form.

If we assume that there is greater wisdom inherent in a learning environment, that the subject is a "Divine Source" that is in the middle of the room teaching all of us, then resistance might also be the subject's teaching. When you experience resistance and you shape shift into third space, the gift is for everyone that's present. Shifting into third space facilitates *everyone's* learning about this subject. In other words, maybe this isn't *really* a conflict between yourself and another person (although it might feel that way). Maybe this is the subject telling you to shift, so that you can allow what wants to emerge, so that the entire group can learn. After all, no matter how much skill or expertise you have, in the greater scheme of things, you're a learner too.

REFLECTING
ON YOUR EXPERIENCE

Creating Space . . .

Are there certain clients or colleagues that you feel more distant from?

What fears underlie your attempt to distance yourself?

How might you work to bridge this distance? List five things you might do...

1.

2.

3.

4.

5.

When you have encountered resistance, how have you responded?

The next time you encounter resistance, how might you try developing third space?

Renewing Inspiration . . .

Try some sentence completions:

> *The reason I started doing this work was...*

> *The gift I bring to this work is...*

> *My biggest worry when I teach (or counsel, mentor, present information) is...*

The thing that gets in my way when I teach is...

What I would like to explore in my teaching is...

I know I am teaching well when...

Planting Seeds . . .

List five changes you would like to make in your work, from the significant to the small.

1.

2.

3.

4.

5.

For each of the changes in the list above, write an action you can take this week.

1.

2.

3.

4.

5.

Tending the field . . .

How do you want to be when you experience criticism?

I want confidence, the ability to be fluid, and an awareness of what's going on, both within me, with the criticizer, and in the room itself.

— a public speaker

Try a sentence completion:

The best way for me to handle criticism is...

For me, criticism from my clients requires that I get recon-
nected with what I'm doing in my work with them. Rather
than get thrown off base by it, I need to be able to hear it and
see if it's valid. Sometimes when I reflect on criticism, it actually
strengthens my own convictions about what I'm doing. But in
other situations, criticism has helped me developed a more bal-
anced and inclusive position.

– health practitioner and workshop leader

Try writing a question to your "inner teacher" and sign it as you would
a standard letter. Address the response to yourself as if you were your
inner teacher.

Dear Inner Teacher,
What am I avoiding in my work?
Mark

Dear Mark,
It's time to take this to the next level. You're ready to shift into
something new. You've been keeping yourself too small.
Sincerely,
Your Inner Teacher

Digging Deeper . . .

If you have a thorny issue that you haven't been able to move past, the method below will help you dig a little deeper. Start by getting out some colored pencils, crayons, or pastels and draw a picture that seems to embody those feelings surrounding the situation. (The drawing doesn't have to be "good" or skillfully done. It's simply meant to get things moving inside yourself.)

After you have completed the picture, jot down about 12 words that seem to arise from it . . .

1.   7.

2.   8.

3.   9.

4.   10.

5.   11.

6.   12.

Write a poem that uses your list of words. Once again the poem does not have to be any good, or even make sense. You won't be showing it to anyone. By letting yourself simply play with your feelings using words as your tool, you can gain surprising insights. "Play" is the operative word here. If this exercise feels like hard work, lighten up a little!

From his drawing, a fitness coach wrote down the words *celebrate, joy, assignments, terror, fear, insanity, enthusiasm*. He wrote the following poem:

"When I coach,
I commit to celebrating my client's achievements,
conveying my genuine enthusiasm.
I will not let terror, fear, or insanity rule."

CONCLUSION
Higher Vision

The greatest friend of the soul is the unknown. Yet we are afraid of the unknown because it lies outside our vision and control. We avoid or quell it by filtering it through our protective barriers of domestication and control. But the normal way never leads home.

— JOHN O'DONOHUE

Rich Life

W.B. YEATS ONCE REMARKED, "Happiness is neither virtue nor pleasure nor this thing or that, but simple growth. We are happy when we are growing." While this book was originally written for adults who teach (broadly defined) as part of their work, teaching and learning occur throughout everyday life. We teach and learn all the time. My love for teaching began when I realized that I could be a *learner* when I teach, and in fact, I was a better teacher when I held that position. My job was to create space and then listen for the higher wisdom that was already present in the situation. To me, it's the ultimate adventure. There is nothing quite like working with other people from a position of "not knowing."

When we teach, we are meeting *life*, in all its various forms. Isn't that what we all want? Rich, meaningful lives? Being willing to dive under issues, exploring myself and others more deeply, being open to new possibilities, experiencing beauty and wonder, are what a rich life is all about. At its best, our work is about something much deeper and more beautiful than mere mechanics or information delivery. The beauty of teaching is not in the outcomes. It is in the richness of the experience itself.

In Chapter One we learned that the foundation for our teaching work is who we are, and in Chapter Two we discovered our passions, developed the skills of discernment and critical thinking, and gained trust in our perceptions. We learned that when we're disconnected from our authentic voice and passions, we're equally disconnected from our intellects. In Chapter Three we opened our imaginations and envisioned possibilities that took us beyond traditional notions of learning. We explored the importance of beauty in learning, expanding our repertoire to include metaphoric connections, diversity, and the wisdom of process.

After opening our imaginations to new possibilities, we were ready to create a sturdy structure for learning in Chapter Four. We discovered the importance of a strong but flexible container when engaging in the messy business of teaching and learning. And in Chapter Five we partnered with the unknown—becoming empty, stepping out of our roles at times, speaking our "truths," giving ourselves definition, and meeting our clients as equals. Finally, in Chapter Six we met challenges and cultivated third space, putting all our learning skills into practice.

Theodore Zeldin wrote that the antidote to fear is not courage. The antidote to fear is curiosity, and that's what I have found to be true. No matter what situation I find myself in, what works for me is to frame it as an experiment that is here for me to learn from. Any difficult situation can be used as a point of inquiry, as a "thing" to be "studied." *What can I learn here?* For myself, teaching has gifted me with many important lessons that I never would have learned in any other way. Every mistake and misadventure has expanded my life, because each was an opportunity for me to learn.

In the last chapter we explored third space. Third space is imaginal space—it's where our higher wisdom resides. Third space gives us a broader view of a particular situation, helping us see what we need to learn, turning the challenge into a journey. The metaphors that we developed for "teaching at our best" are examples of third space. The Inner Bridgings visualization and the *Digging Deeper* exercises (which include visualizations, working with intuition, collage, an inspiration board, poetry, and fairy tales) are also offered as ways to bring you into that place of expanded knowing.

Another way to think of third space is that it provides the *higher vision*. One day when I was in graduate school, I passed a group of people planting flowers on an abandoned rail track that ran through the south side of Chicago where I lived. Their sign read, "Help us build a garden!" and the sight was inspiring and compelling. They weren't just planting flowers or cleaning up trash. Rather, they were *building a garden* in this drab and somewhat dangerous neighborhood. No matter what the situation, our inspiration and growth will always lie in the higher vision. The higher vision is what gives us the energy and enthusiasm to move forward.

A friend who loves metaphors asked me what metaphor came to my mind for this book. My subconscious mind immediately gave me a very clear image, but I didn't want to share it, because my image was the mushroom cloud after the atomic bomb was dropped. (That certainly *was* messy.)

My subconscious had been influenced by a play I saw recently about the science that led up to the bomb. What I remember from watching the play is that two different substances collide which results in the splitting of atoms, and the splitting of atoms creates an enormous amount of energy. Finding myself curious, I looked it up on wikipedia.org:

> In 1898, French physicist Pierre Curie and his Polish wife Maria Sklodowska-Curie had discovered that present in pitchblende, an ore of uranium, was a substance which emitted large amounts of radioactivity, which they named radium. This raised the hopes of both scientists and lay people that the elements around us could contain tremendous amounts of unseen energy, waiting to be tapped.

There is something about the line "containing tremendous amounts of unseen energy, waiting to be tapped" that has to do with why this particular image came up for me. *Getting Messy* is about learning, creativity, imagination, and traversing into unknown space. It presents a higher vision of teaching and learning, a vision that bridges two well-established polarities: learner-expert and learning process-creative process. When we bridge these polarities, we create third space—imaginal space. Like the radium discovered by Pierre and Maria Curie, imaginal space is already present in our everyday lives. It is *unseen energy waiting to be tapped*. I believe it's time for us to tap it.

Teaching and learning are ventures in creativity. We experience the world, chew on our impressions a little bit, and then we offer our own unique expression back in response. *Getting Messy* is simply my contribution to the ongoing conversation. There are many things we still don't know about teaching and learning—why people retain odd bits of information, what causes the quirky diversity in people's interests and curiosities, why interests can shift over time. But while the conversation about teaching and learning is unfinished, I hope this book has helped you to uncover your own response. Your own unique response is what matters, in the end.

REFLECTING
ON YOUR EXPERIENCE

Creating Space . . .

Do you have a sturdy structure that will support your continued learning and growth? Is there anything you can do to make your container more supportive of who you are?

Renewing Inspiration . . .

What has changed for you since we began this process? What ideas have come up that seem important to you? Write down a key thought or piece of advice that you would like to keep in mind to guide you in the future...

Planting Seeds . .

What questions are you still pondering? They can be big questions like, "What's my higher vision for my work?" "What's my purpose when I teach/lead/facilitate/counsel/mentor?" Or small questions like, "How do I handle this disruptive person?"

Tending The field . . .

Who are the people with whom you are having the most difficulties relating at the present time?

In what ways do you think you are being asked to grow in these relationships?

List three characteristics that you most despise in other people.

1.

2.

3.

List three characteristics that you most appreciate in other people.

1.

2.

3.

In what ways are these positive and negative qualities present in you?

Digging Deeper . . .

In Chapter One we received a vision for our teaching work. Now that you have spent time reflecting on your work and exploring what it means to be a learner, let's ask for another image and see what has changed.

Sit or lie in a comfortable position, close your eyes, and focus on your breathing for a few minutes. Ask yourself for an image that represents your current work. Allow the image to come, without censoring it.

Are you in this image? If so, where are you? Are you standing, sitting, flying? What emotion is present for you in this image? If you want advice on some matter, you could imagine that someone has shown up to help you. You can carry the image wherever you would like to go with it, but the important thing is to let it come, rather than forcing it. Ask the image for help, and follow whatever you get.

One workshop participant got the image of his feet being stuck in the mud. He asked the mud how he could get unstuck, and the mud told him that he simply needed to enjoy the mud right now. There was nowhere that he needed to go.

Write a poem or some phrases about what you see. Don't worry about creating a "good" poem, because no one else is going to read it. The point is to let the words come. If you get stuck, just write details of what you see in the image.

Epilogue

In one way or another, I have always been teaching. It all started when I entered first grade. I came home from school and promptly set up shop. My first student was my baby brother Jeff, who was just learning to walk. I pulled him around the living room, pointed to various objects, and instructed him on what they were. "That's a lamp," I said. "That's the davenport." "That's a reclining chair." Jeff looked at me and nodded. He was an attentive student.

Two years later, I declared to Mr. Hall, my third-grade teacher, that *I* would never be a teacher. It was too boring, I explained, having to repeat information over and over again. Mr. Hall told me that teaching wasn't really like that, but I wasn't convinced.

As fate would have it, my first real job when I turned sixteen was teaching. I was hired to be a beginner swim instructor at the city pool. My eighth-grade English teacher, Mrs. Holt, was a student in one of my classes. At the second class, she gulped some water, got scared, and started flailing about. I dived in and rescued her.

Perhaps because of the uncertainness of it, I loved teaching beginners. It was thrilling to see people go from clinging with white knuckles to the side of the pool, to courageously plunging forward into the great expanse of water in front of them, trying their best to do something that sort of looked like a Front crawl. May we all have such courage.

Acknowledgements

Of the many teachers who have contributed to me, I would like to particularly thank Frank Rubenfeld and Howard Schechter for their wisdom about teaching and learning. Over the last ten years, I have sought out their advice, soaked up what they had to tell me, and incorporated many of their insights into this book. Their sharing has not only made me a better teacher, but a better person.

Thank you to my wonderful editor, Leslie Keenan, who helped me in the final stages to get a loose draft of passionate prose into something that could be called a book. I am also grateful to Melissa Anderson, Susan Hermanson, Chris Kagan, Robin Lohans, Jyoti SaeUn, Elka Eastly Vera, and Dorcey Joyce Weaver for their help with issues of book design and layout, and to Viviane Barton, Dakota Bayard, and Karen Leland for content and editorial suggestions. I could not have finished this book without the "mid-wifing" services of graphic designer Leslie Lauf (the book was delighted as well). It was a pleasure and a joy to work with her on the initial concept and layout, and to see my vision for this book become a reality. I was also lucky to meet Susan Adler, who took the author photograph, and I was fortunate to discover the awesome design work of *the*BookDesigners, who did both the cover and the interior design. Lots of talented people contributed to this book, and I am deeply grateful.

And most importantly, I want to thank my students, colleagues, and clients. They've inspired me, pushed me, challenged me, and definitely helped me learn. That's what it's all about.

Bibliography

Abrahamson, Eric and David Freedman. *A Perfect Mess: The Hidden Benefits of Disorder.* New York: Little, Brown and Company, 2008.

Alighieri, Dante. *De Monarchia.* Florence: Rostagno, 921/1317.

Arendt, Hannah. *The Human Condition.* University of Chicago Press, 1958.

Argyris, Chris. *Overcoming Organizational Defenses: Facilitating Organizational Learning.* Englewood Cliffs, NJ: Prentice-Hall, 1990.

Ayers, W. *To Teach: The Journey of a Teacher.* New York, NY: Teachers College Press, 1993.

Baldwin, Christina. *Calling the Circle: The First and Future Culture.* New York: Bantam Books, 1998.

Baldwin, Christina. *Life's Companion: Journal Writing as a Spiritual Practice.* New York: Bantam Books, 1990.

Bayles, David, and Ted Orland. *Art and fear.* Eugene, OR: Image Continuum Press, 2001.

Booth, Eric. *The Everyday Work of Art: Awakening the Extraordinary in Your Daily Life.* Naperville, IL: Sourcebooks, Inc., 1997.

Braddon, Mary E. *Lady Audley's Secret.* Peterborough, Ontario: Broadview, 1862

Brookfield, Stephen. *Becoming a Critically Reflective Teacher.* San Francisco: Jossey-Bass, 1995.

Bruner, Jerome. *Acts of Meaning.* Cambridge, MA: Harvard University Press, 1990.

Buber, Martin. *I and Thou.* Translated by Walter Kaufmann. New York: Charles Scriber's Sons, 1970.

Cameron, Julia. *The Artist's Way: A Spiritual Path to Higher Creativity.* New York: Jeremy P. Tarcher, 1992.

Casey, Caroline. *Making the Gods Work for You: The Astrological Language of the Psyche.* New York: Three Rivers Press, 1998.

Clements, Jennifer; Dorothy Ettling; Diane Jenett; and Lisa Shields. *Organic Inquiry: If Research were Sacred.* Palo Alto: Serpentina Press, 1999.

Corbin, Henri. *Creative Imagination in the Sufism of Ibn 'Arabi.* Princeton, NJ: Princeton University Press, 1969.

Csikszentmihalyi, Mihaly, and Eugene Halton. *The Meaning of Things: Domestic Symbols and the Self.* Cambridge: Cambridge University Press, 1981.

Csikszentmihaly, Mihaly, and Kim Hermanson. Intrinsic Motivation in Museums: Why Does One Want to Learn? Chapter 15 in Hooper-Greenhill, Eilean (ed.) *The Educational Role of the Museum.* New York: Routledge.

Daloz, Laurent A. *Effective Teaching and Mentoring.* San Francisco: Jossey-Bass, 1986.

Del Prete, Thomas. *Thomas Merton and the Education of the Whole Person.* Birmingham, AL: Religious Education Press, 1990.

Dominguez, Joe, and Vicki Robin. *Your Money or Your Life: Transforming Your Relationship with Money and Achieving Financial Independence.* New York: Penguin Press, 1999.

Forest, Ohky S. *Dreaming the Council Ways: True Native Teachings from the Red Lodge.* York Beach, ME: Samuel Weiser, Inc., 2000.

Foss, Martin. Foss, M. *Metaphor and Symbol in Human Experience.* Lincoln, NE: University of Nebraska Press, 1949.

Freeman, Jo. "The Tyranny of Structurelessness." The Second Wave 2, no. 1 (1972).

Gardner, John. On Leadership. New York: Simon & Schuster, 1990.

Goldberg, Natalie. *Wild Mind.* New York: Bantam Books, 1990.

Goleman, Daniel. *Emotional Intelligence: Why It Can Matter More than IQ.* New York: Bantam Books, 1995.

Grandin, Temple. *Thinking in Pictures: and Other Reports from my Life with Autism.* New York: Vintage Books, 1995.

Greenleaf, Robert. *Servant Leadership: A Journey into the Nature of Legitimate Power and Greatness.* New York: Paulist Press, 1977.

Gress, J. R. *Curriculum: An Introduction to the Field*. Berkeley: McCutchen Publishing, 1978.

Habermas, Jurgen. *The Theory of Communicative Action*. Vol. 2. Oxford, England: Polity Press, 1987.

Hadamard, Jacques. *An Essay on the Psychology of Invention in the Mathematical Field*. Princeton: Princeton University Press, 1945.

Heider, John. *The Tao of Leadership: Lau Tzu's Tao Te Ching Adapted for a New Age*. Atlanta, GA: Humanics Limited, 1985.

Hillman, James. *The Soul's Code: In Search of Character and Calling*. New York: Warner Books, 1996.

Jaworski, Joseph. *Synchronicity: The Inner Path of Leadership*. San Francisco: Berrett-Koehler Publishers, 1996.

Johnson, Robert. *Balancing Heaven & Earth*. San Francisco: Harper Collins, 1998

Johnston, Charles M. *Necessary Wisdom: Meeting the Challenge of a New Cultural Maturity*. Berkeley: ICD Press, 1991.

Jolande, Jacobi, ed. *C. G. Jung: Psychological Reflections: A New Anthology of His Writings*. London: Routledge and Kegan Paul, 1971.

Jung, Carl Gustav. "Commentary on 'The Secret of the Golden Flower," in *Collected Works of Carl Jung* volume 13. Princeton: Princeton University Press, 1967.

King, Laurie R. *A Letter of Mary*. New York: St. Martin's Press, 1996.

Kingsley, Peter. "In the Dark Places of Wisdom." *Parabola* 23, no. 4 (1998).

Krishnamurti, J. *Education and the Significance of Life*. New York: Harper & Row, 1953.

Krishnamurti, J. *Think on These Things*. New York: Harper & Row, 1964.

Kunitz, Stanley. *Next-to-Last-Things: New Poems and Essays*. Boston: Atlantic Monthly Press, 1986.

Lafrance, Danielle. *Berkeley! A Literary Tribute*. Berkeley: Heyday Books, 1997.

Lakoff, George, and Mark Johnson. *Metaphors We Live By*. Chicago: The University of Chicago Press, 1980.

Lamm, Z. "The Status of Knowledge in the Radical Concept of Education," in *Curriculum: An Introduction to the Field*. Edited by John Gress. Berkeley: McCutchen Publishing, 1978.

Livsey, Rachel. *The Courage to Teach: A Guide for Reflection and Renewal*. San Francisco: Jossey-Bass, 1999.

London, Peter. *No More Secondhand Art*. New York: Shambhala Publications, Inc., 1989.

Merton, Thomas. "The Poorer Means: A Meditation on Ways to Unity," in *Sobornost*, Winter-Spring (1966).

Milne, A.A. *Winnie-the-Pooh 80th Anniversary Edition*. New York: Penguin Group, 2006.

Mindell, Arnold. *The Leader as Martial Artist: An Introduction to Deep Democracy*. Portland, OR: Lao Tse Press, 2000.

Oliver, Donald. *Education and Community: A Radical Critique of Innovative Schooling*. New York: Harper & Row, 1976.

Palmer, Parker. *The Courage to Teach: Exploring the Inner Landscape of a Teacher's Life*. San Francisco: Jossey-Bass, 1998.

Peck, M. Scott. *The Road Less Traveled and Beyond: Spiritual Growth in an Age of Anxiety*. New York: Simon & Schuster, 1978.

Peck, M. Scott. *The Different Drum: Community Making and Peace*. New York: Simon & Schuster, 1987.

Peck, M. Scott. *A World Waiting to be Born: Civility Rediscovered*. New York: Bantam Books, 1994.

Premack, David, and Ann Premack. *Original Intelligence: Unlocking the Mystery of Who We Are*. New York: McGraw-Hill, 2002.

Samples, Bob. *The Metaphoric Mind: A Celebration of Creative Consciousness*. New York: Addison-Wesley Publishing Company, 1976.

Schechter, Howard. *Jupiter's Rings: Balance from the Inside Out*. Ashland, Oregon: White Cloud Press, 2002.

Sloan, Douglas. *Insight and Imagination: The Emancipation of Thought and the Modern World*. Westport, CN: Charles F. Kettering Foundation, 1983.

Starhawk. *Truth or Dare: Encounters with Power, Authority, and Mystery*. New York: Harper Collins, 1987.

Steffens, Lincoln. *The Autobiography of Lincoln Steffens.* New York: Harcourt Brace & Company, 1931.

Tieger, Paul, and Barbara Barron. *Do What You Are: Discover the Perfect Career for You Through the Secrets of Personality Type.* Boston: Little, Brown, 1995.

Vaughan, Frances. *Awakening Intuition.* New York: Anchor Books, 1978.

Waite, Robert. *The Psychopathic God.* New York: Da Capo Press, 1993.

Warnock, Mary. *Imagination.* London: Faber & Faber Press, 1976.

Weil, Simone. *Waiting for God.* New York: G.P. Putnam's Sons, 1951.

Woolf, Virgina. *A Room of One's Own.* New York: Harcourt Brace, 1929.

Zeldin, Theodore. *An Intimate History of Humanity.* New York: HarperCollins, 1994.

About the Author

Kim Hermanson, Ph.D., is on the faculty of the Sophia Center at Holy Names University and Meridian University. She has taught courses and seminars at the University of California Berkeley Extension, the Institute of Transpersonal Psychology, Flathead Valley Community College, Esalen Institute, and Vista College. Learning and the creative process have been continual themes in Kim's classes and published work. In 2006 her first book, *Sky's the Limit: The Art of Nancy Dunlop Cawdrey*, received an Honorable Mention from the Independent Publisher Book Awards. Other noteworthy publications include a popular article and book chapter on learning in museums "Intrinsic Motivation in Museums: What Makes Visitors Want to Learn?" with Mihaly Csikszentmihalyi, author of the classic *Flow: The Psychology of Optimal Experience*; and an article on educational indicators with Tony Bryk, the current President of the Carnegie Foundation, that was subsequently included as a chapter in the *Review of Research in Education*. For her doctoral work at the University of Chicago, Kim studied how adults learn in everyday life. An early version of her doctoral dissertation received an Outstanding Research Award from the Holistic Education sub-group of the American Educational Research Association.

KimHermanson.com
Learn more about the author
and purchase additional copies of *Getting Messy*.

Made in the USA
Columbia, SC
24 February 2018